Milestone Planning for Successful Ventures

QuickStart for Windows

Milestone Planning for Successful Ventures
QuickStart for Windows

Bernard J. David
Lecturer in Entrepreneurship
The Wharton School, University of Pennsylvania

Contribution from
Zenas Block, Adjunct Professor and Senior Research Associate,
Center for Entrepreneurial Studies, Stern School of Business, New York University
Adjunct Professor, Rensselaer Polytechnic Institute—School of Management

boyd & fraser publishing company

I(T)P   An International Thomson Publishing Company

Danvers • Albany • Bonn • Boston • Cincinnati • Detroit • London • Madrid • Melbourne
Mexico City • New York • Paris • San Francisco • Singapore • Tokyo • Toronto • Washington

Executive Editor/Acquisitions Editor: DeVilla Williams
Project Manager/Developmental Editor: Abigail Reip
Production Editor: Jackie Bedoya
Production Services, Composition, and Interior Design: Elm Street Publishing Services, Inc.
Cover Design: Michael Rogondino
Cover Photo: Tom Collicott
Manufacturing Coordinator: Gordon Woodside
Marketing Coordinator: Karen Grantham

Distributed by boyd & fraser publishing company
A division of International Thomson Publishing, Inc.

I(T)P   The ITP logo is a trademark under license.

© Educational Software, Inc.

Printed in the United States of America

For more information, contact boyd & fraser publishing company:

boyd & fraser publishing company
One Corporate Place • Ferncroft Village
Danvers, Massachusetts 01923, USA

International Thomson Publishing Europe
Berkshire House 168–173
High Holborn
London, WC1V 7AA, England

Thomas Nelson Australia
102 Dodds Street
South Melbourne 3205
Victoria, Australia

Nelson Canada
1120 Birchmont Road
Scarborough, Ontario
Canada M1K 5G4

International Thomson Editores
Campose Eliscos 385, Piso 7
Col. Polanco
11560 Mexico D.F. Mexico

International Thomson Publishing GmbH
Konigswinterer Strasse 418
53227 Bonn, Germany

International Thomson Publishing Asia
221 Henderson Road
#05–10 Henderson Building
Singapore 0315

International Thomson Publishing Japan
Hirakawacho Kyowa Building, 3F
2–2–1 Hirakawacho
Chiyoda-ku, Tokyo 102, Japan

1 2 3 4 5 6 7 8 9 10 M 8 7 6 5 4

Library of Congress Cataloging-in-Publication Data:

David, Bernard J.
    Milestone planning for successful ventures / by Bernard J. David ;
contribution from Zenas Block.—1st ed.
    p.   cm.
  ISBN 0–89426–860–0 (softcover).—ISBN 0-89426-861-9 (softcover).
  —ISBN 0-89426-223-8 (softcover).—ISBN 0-89426-222-X (softcover)
    1. New business enterprises—United States—Planning. 2. New
business enterprises—United States—Planning—Case studies.
I. Block, Zenas. II. Title.
HD62.5.D37   1994
  658.1'1—dc20

94-29642

The Milestone Planning for Successful Ventures™ paradigm is intended for use in the planning and monitoring of new ventures. It incorporates the ability to establish assumptions in venture planning and monitoring; test those assumptions in milestones; assign levels of involvement to various individuals (i.e., responsibility, veto, support, information); establish estimated and actual timeframes for milestone completion; and set forth estimated and real costs of the milestones.

The paradigm has been translated into software. The software was developed with four parameters.

1. *Easy to use.* People who use this software don't want to be bothered by the technical elements of the program.

2. *Powerful.* If it doesn't enable the user to garner new information in a fashion he or she couldn't previously achieve, it will not meet its objective of being a powerful decision-making tool.

3. *Flexible.* All ventures that will be planned and monitored with this software will be dynamic in nature—they will change many times in their evolution as ventures. In order to facilitate this process, the Milestone Planning for Successful Ventures™ software must possess a tremendous amount of flexibility.

4. *Based on real world needs.* The software must be practical and usable for real businesses. While it may reflect some academic theories, it should do so only as they may be practically applied to real situations that exist in the planning and monitoring of new ventures.

This book takes you through the paradigm; introduces many cases in which you can test your skills in the paradigm's execution; and gives you a window to its computer-based implementation with the Milestone Planning for Successful Ventures™ software program.

ACKNOWLEDGMENTS

My deepest thanks to Richard Chang, a former student and friend, for his assistance in writing The Spice Kitchen case.

Bernard J. David is deeply involved in the planning and creation of a venture that will introduce smart cards used as "Stored Value Cards" to automate low value coin and currency transactions in the world payment system.

David is the owner of a company that specializes in planning and implementing technology to be used for a strategic business advantage. He also owns Educational Software, Inc., a company formed to develop and market software born in the university environment.

David is the author of a host of articles, published or referenced by *datapro, Systems 3x/AS/400, Midrange Systems, ComputerWorld, Macintosh Buyer's Guide, Computer & Software News, InfoWorld, PC Magazine, PC Week, MacWorld, Profit Computing, The Office, The Word, USA Today, Business Week, The Delaware State Chamber Business Journal,* and *The Wall Street Journal.*

David is the author of *The Entrepreneurial PC (First and Second Editions)* published by McGraw-Hill. He is co-author of *Dvorak's Inside Track to the Macintosh,* also published by McGraw-Hill, and *The Mac Shareware Emporium* (Simon & Schuster, Inc.).

Bernard J. David is a Lecturer in the Management Department at The Wharton School, University of Pennsylvania. He holds both a Bachelor of Science and an M.B.A. from the Wharton School, University of Pennsylvania. He also holds a Bachelor of Arts in Political Science from the University of Pennsylvania.

David serves on the Board of Directors of four companies.

CONTENTS

Chapter 1   A Framework for Milestone Planning   1

Appendix   Assumptions: Examples of the Most Common Types   21

Chapter 2   The Sandbox and Ting Case   25

Chapter 3   The Spice Kitchen Case (A)   29

Chapter 4   The Spice Kitchen Case (B)   47

Chapter 5   The MaxRail, Ltd. Case   61

Chapter 6   The Enviromarine Corp. Case   83

Chapter 7   Milestone Planning for Successful Ventures: QuickStart   97

Milestone Planning for Successful Ventures   98

Before You Start   99

Requirements   99

Installing Milestone Planning for Successful Ventures   100

Milestones   101

Using Milestone Planning for Successful Ventures   103

Reporting   132

Index   151

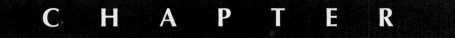

CHAPTER

1

A FRAMEWORK FOR
MILESTONE PLANNING
by Zenas Block

Planning for new businesses or ventures is a totally different ball game than planning for established businesses. The fundamental reasons are very simple.

New venture planning is primarily based on assumptions.
Established business planning is primarily based on facts.
Established businesses have a track record, new ones don't.
New ventures rarely go according to plan.
Established businesses more often do.

The purpose of a business plan for a going business is to provide a blueprint for getting from here to there in a specific time period. The tasks and objectives of participants are known. There is knowledge of existing competition. Reasonable predictions can be made based on past experience. The myriad of details ranging from quality needs, performance requirements of products or services, ability of people, and best suppliers, to production, distribution, and selling costs and capacity—all the details that make it possible to assemble projections and budgets people can be expected to meet—are present.

Yet, in spite of all this information, turbulence in the environment, new competition, technology advances, and the loss of key people can derail the best plans of well-managed established companies.

In answer to the question: "How are you folks doing?" How often have we heard, or indeed replied: "We're meeting our projections", as if that were an answer to the question. That really answers another question: "How close have you come to your projections?"

Why are we so focused on meeting projections? By and large, reward systems are keyed to this; managers are judged by how well they can plan and meet the plan. Credibility is established or destroyed by the track record of a manager in meeting plans and projections.

Projections for new ventures based on traditional planning methods are nothing but exercises in fantasy based mainly on

Note: This chapter is an expansion of the planning chapter in *Corporate Venturing: Creating New Businesses Within the Firm*, HBR Press (1993) by Z. Block and I. A. MacMillan, to be published in *Milestone Planning for Successful Ventures*, edited by Bernard J. David (Boyd & Fraser Publishing).

assumptions, and few facts. Thus, the criterion for meeting projections as a basis for judging performance is somewhat ludicrous. When they are met, the event might be considered a statistically improbable accident, or based on a projection so conservative that it would be difficult not to meet.

The fact is that plans and projections for new businesses have no relationship to the realities that ultimately occur. Even worse news is that efforts to meet original plans when emerging reality screams that the events and objectives that are planned are not valid result in massive expenditures and losses, and the effort itself is a primary cause of new venture failure.

Our mass hypnosis on the role of planning causes events like these to occur: In September 1987 a new venture for a computer hardware enhancement was financed by venture capital. The target market entry date was September 1988. In order to meet that date, development was to be completed by June 1988, by which time a manufacturing facility was to be ready. The market entry was planned to be national in scope, and regional offices with trained staff were to be in place by September 1988. The only thing that met schedule was the existence of regional offices with staff. Development was not completed by June, nor by September. The company could not get zoning approval for their plant on the selected site. The burn rate of the venture was running at about $500,000 per month. The company finally began with an outside manufacturer producing a product that was not like the one originally intended, at the end of 1988.

Other well-known examples of new venture disasters are Polarvision (the Polaroid motion picture camera) Federal Express's Zapmail, and Exxon's oil shale project.

The problem common to all of these ventures was the presence of assumptions, either conscious or not, which were wrong; yet actions continued that ignored the emerging visibility of their fallacy.

WHY PLAN AT ALL?

In light of this experience, is it really possible to plan effectively for new ventures? Certainly not by using traditional planning methods. If planning is to be done, it must be based on the reality of new business formation, which is simply that we don't know what will happen, when it will happen, and how much it will cost. Starting a new business is truly an experiment based on a hypothesis. (For example, starting a fast-food restaurant chain serving fast, healthy foods is based on the hypothesis that there are enough people actually near or passing by the intended locations who will buy enough fast, healthy foods to support a business.)

Experiments are designed to learn something, and thus the dominant concept in new venture planning is to generate an action plan designed to produce forced learning, as well as steps toward realization of a goal. Learning is essential in order to replace hypotheses (assumptions) with facts or better assumptions. The learning must be applied to future planned actions, no matter what earlier plans may have articulated, in order to move toward realization of the goal. This means that the action plan for the venture will be changing quite often, a fact to be applauded as evidence of adaptation to reality.

Thus the rationale and the method of planning for new ventures converge: we need to plan in order to learn what to do, and the method of planning must be one that produces the learning that tells us what to do.

The building blocks that provide the elements of new venture planning are assumptions, milestones, and critical path design resulting in critical path milestone planning (CPMP).

This chapter will outline how to use milestone planning to test assumptions while moving the fledgling business toward survival and profitability or to minimize losses if the basic assumptions on which the business is based are found to be invalid.

SOME DEFINITIONS

Assumption: a belief about facts and relationships unknown at the time the belief is expressed. Examples include:

The *market* will grow to $100 million in three years.
The prime rate will remain below 7 percent for two years.
The price of oil will stay at $32 per barrel.
The elapsed time from a first sales call to an order will be 90 days.

Customers will pay our planned prices.

Our cost per unit will be as planned.

Milestone: a completed task or event, or the achievement of a condition or status, or a specific point in time. Examples are:

The concept test will be completed by October 17, 1994.

Pilot production runs will begin on March 3 and be completed by April 15, 1995.

Material cost estimates will be confirmed by February 9.

Critical Path: a sequence of actions or events where each succeeding event is dependent on the completion of the preceding event or can be pursued in parallel with another event, which will be required as precedent for a following event.

Critical Path Milestone Planning: the planning of milestone events and their completion, which takes into account the dependency of each event on the completion of others by designing the sequence in which they will occur. For example, product development will begin when the concept test has been completed if the concept test verifies our basic market acceptance assumption. Product development objectives will take into account what is learned from the concept test. The relationship between these components is shown in the framework described below.

THE BASIC FRAMEWORK

1. The most important assumptions about a proposed venture are articulated and actions to test them are designed.

2. The important events to be completed and intermediate stages to be reached are defined.

3. The sequence in which each of the above can or must be done is determined, thus establishing a critical milestone path.

4. These are woven into the business plan and scenario which will be used.

5. At the completion of each milestone, review occurs to determine what changes must be made in order to accomplish the basic goal, or to change the goal, or to abort.

Inherent in this approach is the knowledge that some assumptions will require replacement with facts or a better assumption, which will alter the events that require completion and the sequence in which they can occur, thus requiring changes in the plan and activity scenario.

ASSUMPTION TYPES

The identification of the important assumptions is the heart of this process. They are the statements of hypotheses upon which the venture is based. While there may be dozens, or even hundreds of assumptions, it is first important to identify those that fit the statement: "If this assumption is not true, then there is no reason for going into this business" or "if this assumption is found to be untrue, then we will get out of this business." These are the **go/no go** assumptions upon which the business concept is completely dependent, (i.e., if the assumption is not true, there is no basis for the business).

Then, there are the **high impact** assumptions: those that seriously affect the timing, costs, and other factors that make the venture more or less attractive.

Finally, there are the **relatively minor** assumptions that are similar to high-impact assumptions except that the consequences of invalidity are not catastrophic, but nevertheless affect the planned actions.

In the process of identifying assumptions, two principal hazards are present:

1. Making so many assumptions that the entire process becomes absurdly cumbersome and unmanageable.
2. Failing to articulate and recognize go/no go assumptions.

An example of the latter characterized Exxon's entry into the oil shale recovery business. The *stated assumption* on which the business was based was that the price of oil would stay over $30 per barrel. Exxon exited the business after a $4 billion loss when oil prices dropped significantly. Exxon made either an *unconscious or unstated assumption* that energy conservation efforts during the late 1970's would not affect oil consumption and that OPEC would continue to control supply to hold the price up. In fact, oil demand and oil prices did drop.

Consider what might have been done had Exxon known or articulated these latter assumptions. Certainly consumption could be tracked on a month-to-month basis to see whether there was any drop in demand. Assumption statement: Oil demand will not drop as a result of conservation efforts. Test: Follow oil consumption demand every month for 6 to 12 months or every quarter for a year to see whether that assumption is correct. Review oil shale decision at each check point.

HOW TO IDENTIFY AND DEFINE ASSUMPTIONS

In this section we go through each area about which assumptions are made, whether articulated or not, whether conscious or not. Use this as a check list. We also note the probable classification of the assumption, (i.e., whether go/no go, high impact, or relatively minor).

Market and Marketing Assumptions

Who will buy, how much, and why	Go/no go
Usage rate	High impact
Future market growth rate	Depends on the venture
Selling and marketing costs	High impact-Go/no go
Selling cycle time	High impact
Market penetration rate	(Depends on the venture)
Market size	Go/no go-must be enough
Pricing validity	High impact

The size of existing markets is usually determinable. However, if a new product or device is offered as a replacement in an existing market, a go/no go assumption is or should be made concerning the sales or share achievable in a time frame, with intermediate levels achieved along the way. The market testing stage is a point at which that assumption can be tested and modified and further tested during the early market entry period.

If the market is to be developed or if it is in its early stages of development, the assumption is totally dependent on the fact that there is no valid way to predict sales or share in a predictable time period.

Concentration in a limited segment (perhaps geographical) might be used to develop the pattern for rollout based on knowledge obtained in that way. In the earliest stages, before marketing or product development, concept testing in focus groups and interviews with potential customers are used.

In case of new and developing markets, we face the dilemma of either standing by to watch the rate of development and missing out, or diving in and sweating out the slow development of the market. There is no way to "test" the assumption about the rate of market development, other than to either watch or enter, choosing an affordable but effective entry strategy.

Selling cycle time is commonly underestimated with serious consequences when capital is limited, or in a corporate environment where expectations have been developed based on projections with an invalid assumption. One way to test such an assumption is to learn who makes the buying decisions and who can stop them, how annual budgets of the customer affect the timing of such decisions, especially in the case of major expenditures.

Product Assumptions

Product function meets market need	Go/no go
Service requirement	High impact
Quality and uniformity suitability	Go/no go
Product costs	Go/no go
Economic value to customer	High impact
Competitive comparison	High impact
Proprietary protection	High impact

Each of the above areas about which assumptions are made can have relatively minor impact or completely invalidate a business, depending on the intensity of the market need, the nature of competition, and resources available. A new product may not supply all of the anticipated functions intended, but still may be superior to existing products in use. In the case of a small company with limited resources, proprietary protection in the form of strong patents may be an absolute go/no go assumption, which would not be the case for a company with ample resources.

Competitive Assumptions
Identity of present and future competitors
Expected competitive response
Customer switching costs
Competitors' costs
Competitive insulation will exist long enough

Assumptions made about competition will affect entry strategy and operating decisions rather than determine whether or not to continue the business. The impact of competitive action in a niche product/market is less likely to be significant if your entry is the first effective entry into that market. One element can affect go/no go and that is switching costs to the customer. This is precisely why software companies work so hard to get a rapid installed base.

What is particularly important is to design events that can produce signals about competitor intentions. For example, the XYZ company launched a patent licensing venture that required a minimum royalty payment and a minimum license period. They were concerned about response from a specific competitor. XYZ therefore approached a loyal customer of their competitor and proposed a license agreement to that customer knowing full well that they would immediately advise the competitor and would certainly not become a licensee of XYZ.

The competitor responded by stating that they would offer a competing process within three months without requiring a royalty. XYZ immediately modified its license agreement to make it cancelable at any time there was a process that did not infringe and that the licensee wished to use instead. This stopped the competitor dead in its tracks and no competitive process appeared in three months nor for the life of the patent.

Organizational Assumptions
Qualified entrepreneurial management will be available.
Parent support will be sufficient.
Organizational positioning will be a positive factor.
A competent venture team will be assembled.
Bureaucratic obstacles can be overcome.

Another way of looking at organizational assumptions is to ask these questions: What are the essential factors that will produce success in the proposed venture, particularly the knowledge, skills, experience, and know-how required? Do we have or can we supply the factors required? These and the assumptions surrounding the availability of other success factors must be tested and verified. While none are initially go/no go, except for the availability of qualified entrepreneurial management, all are high impact, which affect the course of the venture.

Technology Assumptions

Development time and cost	Go/no go
Proprietary position and duration	Variable
Support know-how and availability	High impact
Production capacity sufficient	High impact
Obsolescence threat acceptable	Go/no go

Development time and cost estimates in a business plan are rarely close to accurate. Ventures related to the creation of a new and promising industry with enormous market potential (e.g., biotechnology, the semiconductor industry early on) may justify virtually any development cost if the money is available. This is not the case for ventures in more limited markets. In either case, the assumption regarding development costs should be broken down into intermediate assumptions, which correspond to phases or stages of the development process.

At the completion of each stage, the overall development assumption may be reviewed to determine go/no go, slow down, speed up, strategic alliance, or any other legitimate alternative to deal with the revealed facts. The development process should use critical path milestone planning. In fact, CPMP was introduced in order to improve the planning and performance of complex, multistep development projects—the NASA moonflight for example!

Economic Assumptions

Break-even sales level	Go/no go or high impact
Cash required to reach breakeven	Variable
Gross margins	Go/no go or high impact
Net margin	Go/no go or high impact
Interest rates	Variable
Cash flow versus time	High impact
Upside potential sales and profit	Go/no go
Downside risk	Go/no go

These are the numbers that determine the worth of the venture and its economic viability. If the break-even sales level required represents an unachievable market share, then clearly the business is a no go. If the assumptions of gross and net margins turn out to be unachievable and the upside potential becomes too low to be worthwhile, the venture may be abandoned or sold to a firm that finds it worthwhile. (Coca-Cola entered the wine business in the 1970s, found that they were unable to achieve the returns they had targeted, and although the business was profitable, disposed of it.)

By clearly identifying the losses expected at sales levels below breakeven, venture management can determine well before expected breakeven is reached whether the expectation is likely to be met. For example: Assume break-even sales will be $2.5 million per month, with fixed costs at $500,000 per month and contribution margin before fixed costs is 20 percent. At sales of $500,000 per month, the loss should be $400,000; at $1 million sales, the loss should be $300,000.

By setting a milestone at 25 percent of break-even sales, and testing the assumption at that point, we can see whether we are on the way to expected breakeven or we need to correct something. If losses are significantly greater than expected, we must learn whether it is due to a factor that must now be built in and will affect the viability of the business for the long run, or whether it simply is taking longer than expected to get variable costs in line with plan.

Environmental Assumptions

The economy will be satisfactory.
Interest rates will be affordable.
No health or safety hazards will threaten or destroy the business.
International relations will not impact the business negatively.
Taxation and government regulations will not adversely affect the business.
There will be a sufficient supply of employees.
There will be no major change in weather.

The assumptions regarding most environmental factors are likely to affect timing, costs, or location rather than whether or not to proceed with a new venture. Yet, Exxon's oil shale venture was dependent on OPEC's high prices; many real estate partnerships were dependent on tax regulations that changed; plenty of ski resorts depended on constant weather that wasn't; the sodium nitrite cancer scare, and the salt/high blood pressure relationship has affected the smoked and cured meat business—in some cases producing the need for new products.

Some Universal Milestones

While each venture has its unique milestone events that must be completed, there are a number that are universal. They are presented here in an idealized form, that is, as if the venturing firm is able to go through each step in the sequence shown without concern about competitive action. Clearly, there are many occasions when this idealized sequence will be bypassed because of a limited window of opportunity, a competitive race, stakes so large, or competitors so large and hot on the trail that the risks incurred are worth it.

Milestone 1—Concept Test

The concept test is the lowest cost stage of any venture, and the first point at which the concept of the product or service, emphasizing its proposed use or functions, can be tested in a sample of the target market. This test can never give a definite "yes" answer, but it can indicate a strong "no," or need for concept modification. Some methods used for concept testing are:

In-Depth Personal Interviews. Personal interviews with potential customers are especially useful for industrial or commercial products or services to ascertain whether there is a perceived need or want for the proposed product. This method is particularly useful where a potential business or product can be built with a relatively small number of large users.

The Focus Group. A group of six to eight members of the target market are stimulated to discuss a product, concept, or need by a trained moderator. Discussion is guided to elicit objections, modifications, or indications of interest in the concept.

Formal Surveys. Written questionnaires with or without telephone interviews addressed to a larger sample of the target market is particularly important for products that are to be marketed to consumers or large numbers of commercial or industrial users. A large enough sample must be used to make statistically valid projections possible. While the results obtained are by no means a predictor of later results, they can provide a more reliable sense of the potentialities—both up and downside.

Milestone 2—Product Test

The purpose of this test is to determine whether there is a match between the concept and the product. The product need not be completely developed, and may be a handmade model or a manually operated service for test purposes. For example, a food company had developed a process for forming many food shapes from chopped material, including bits of chicken meat removed from bones. A product was conceived: A chicken drumstick with no bones and no waste. The concept tested in a focus group of homemakers. It was enthusiastically received. Since the development of machinery to produce this product was expected to be very expensive, a handmade sample of product was produced and a product test was performed with the same focus group. It was totally rejected because of the strangeness of the texture as compared to normal drumstick meat. The project was not continued.

Milestone 3—Feasibility Study

The purpose of this step is to answer these questions:

What will it take to develop the product/service?
What will it cost to develop, manufacture, distribute, sell, service?
Can our firm provide what is necessary?
Will it be worth the effort?

The concept study output can be a trigger to produce financing for conducting a feasibility study, if necessary.

Milestone 4—Prepare the Business Plan

Completion of this milestone will be needed to obtain development financing. The information obtained in the feasibility study and in the concept and product test is used to prepare the plan and build on the many remaining assumptions. It is also a key point at which unconscious assumptions can be discovered through the use of knowledgeable people who are not involved in the preparation of the plan or have no vested interest in the outcome.

Milestone 5—First Financing

Once the prototype is complete, it may then appear that there is merit to the concept or product. And, in order to go further with the venture, it now becomes time to put some financial resources into the project. Or, in order to finish the prototype, it may be necessary to get financing because the prototype itself can't be bootstrapped.

This milestone can be a litmus test for the project or the venture in that even if a concept test shows positive interest and a prototype is built, getting a party to put financing into it shows a certain level of commitment. The financing milestone may take much longer to complete than initially anticipated.

Milestone 6—Product Development

The completion of this milestone will further verify, challenge, or replace the assumptions regarding product functions, performance, and costs that served as the basis for beginning the project in the first place. It will also affect the estimates arrived at through the feasibility study and thus the entire business plan, which will require modification. For major projects, internal milestones for product development require definition as well. These sub milestones can be built from answers to these questions, for example:

What information is needed in order to complete the product?

What components require design and completion before the total product can be assembled?

In what sequence are those components or modules required in order to proceed from step to step?

What regulatory clearances are required?

The outcome of product development will be used to obtain financing for pilot operations and market testing.

Milestone 7—Pilot Test

The pilot test step is always desirable in some form and is often absolutely essential. A small facility is built or found to produce small quantities of product or service that can be used to conduct market tests. It determines whether the data obtained in development can be applied in practice, and further tests whether the assumptions regarding costs, quality, production rates, rejects, and so forth are valid or require change.

The results from this activity will be used to trigger release of funds for the next step—building a plant (or service facility).

Milestone 8—Initial Market Test

Products produced from pilot operations can be used for conducting market tests. The purpose of this step is to test the assumptions regarding the marketing mix (direct selling, advertising, promotion, etc.) required to achieve the assumed market penetration, and the response from samples of the target market to real product at real prices. This is the time to change assumptions to be consistent with the facts learned from this milestone, and to test the new assumptions if necessary.

Milestone 9—Building a Plant

The results of the pilot operation and the initial market test will affect the plant building decision and capacity to be built. Ideally, the decision should wait until the confirmation of the go/no go assumptions or satisfactory replacements have been verified. In actuality, the existing or potential competition may require that many preliminary steps are taken—selecting location, acquiring land, getting zoning clearance, design, etc. However, these steps will be minimized if the results of assumptions tested in pilot and initial market test stage are considered before construction begins.

Milestone 10—Production Start Up

All of the assumptions originally made about production costs, achievable quality, capacity, rejects, and achievable specifications are now finally tested. The key problem with successful products from a marketing viewpoint can be inability to produce sufficiently. The dual effort of meeting commitments for delivery and controlling commitments made, is the challenge at this stage. One assumption that is commonly wrong is the estimate of costs to build a plant and its startup costs. By the time this is realized, it is too late to revise the assumption, but contingency financing should be anticipated and hopefully achieved.

MILESTONES THAT CAN OCCUR AT ANY TIME

The Bellwether Sale

A single sale that enhances credibility to the product, service and company. As an example, for a telecommunications product, a sale to AT&T is a sale to a company that is widely recognized as a leader in its field and careful in its choice of suppliers. Failure to achieve such a sale may be an important signal for redirection or modification of the venture.

The First Significant Price Change

This can result from competitive action and may challenge the assumptions regarding price and therefore margins, or from higher costs than anticipated. Conversely, the change may be triggered by achieving lower costs than assumed and the decision to lower prices to increase rate of market penetration. Discovering unexpected values in the product or service may justify price increases to reflect those values.

First Redesign or Redirection

Either of these actions can be stimulated by revelations in the marketplace or improvements in technology. (A food product originally assumed to be attractive only to the food service market was surprisingly found to be attractive to the direct consumer market and as a consequence, the venture has redirected its marketing resources to exploit that discovery.)

First Competitive Response

Assumptions about competitive response may be invalidated by actual response. Tests to trigger competitive response may be designed to avoid surprises. On the other hand, a strategy to minimize expected response, such as a guerrilla entry strategy, might be considered.

Milestones and Sub Milestones

For the sake of simplicity and manageability, keep the major milestones limited to no more than ten.

To back up these milestones with the support needed, sub milestones may be used, for example, in the concept testing process, each step can be described as a sub milestone, for example, focus group, direct interviews, formal survey.

SUMMARIZING THE BASIC FRAMEWORK FOR MILESTONE PLANNING

1. The most important assumptions (Go/No Go and High Impact) about a proposed venture are articulated and actions to test them designed.

2. The important events to be completed and the intermediate stages to be reached are defined (Milestones).

3. The sequence in which each of the above can or must be done is determined, thus establishing a critical milestone path.

4. These are woven into the business plan and action scenario.

5. At the completion of each milestone, a review of the original assumption and whether and how it must be changed to meet the basic goal is made. If a go/no go assumption or a high impact assumption is found to be invalid, a choice must be made to redirect, change the goal, or abort the venture.

It is virtually impossible that every major assumption made about a venture is originally correct. Plans will require change based on what is learned. Failure to do so will result in unnecessary costs or outright failure. Learning and applying the learning will increase the chances and the magnitude of success.

THE FINDINGS

Once an assumption is tested in a major or sub milestone, you discover certain things—you find out you were correct in your assumptions and the venture should continue on in a given direction, or you learn that some or all of your assumptions were incorrect and that you must change what you initially thought would work.

Given that the world is dynamic, the findings may change over time. And, what seemed correct may turn out to be incorrect over time. The opposite may also happen.

Whatever the case may be, the venture or project may need to be redirected based on your findings. You should redirect it if you find it to be relevant to do so.

RESOURCES

In order to execute any process-based major or sub milestone, people, funds, and time are needed.

People

People are involved in process-based major or sub milestones from two perspectives—either they have primary responsibility for the venture or they are involved in its execution.

Primary Responsibility   If an individual has primary responsibility for completion of a major or sub milestone, the responsibility to complete the major or sub milestone lies on his/her shoulders.

Involvements   People may be involved in a project or venture but not have primary responsibility for it. As such, they may be involved as an individual who has approval or veto of an action, technical approval or veto, who gives required support, or who is a participant in an information loop.

Cost (Planned/Actual)

The second resource to be allocated on a major or sub milestone basis is cost. It is necessary to understand cost to see how the venture is progressing. Before commencing with a given major or sub milestone, you can only estimate what costs are involved. Once you've completed that major or sub milestone, it becomes clear what the actual costs are. Cost can drive the direction of a venture. If you have limited resources, you may find yourself redirecting the venture. Tracking actual versus planned costs can also give you a better sense as to how accurately you can predict this variable.

Time

The dimension of time is an interesting one as it relates to both major and sub milestones. The only thing that matters is the amount of time actually spent on completing a major or sub milestone. The elapsed time is not as relevant as the actual time spent on it. In the real world, though, elapsed time is important. This is the measure by which so many projects or ventures are judged. With an increasing need to compete against time, both actual time spent and elapsed time are good measures to judge performance. In many instances, actual time spent should equal elapsed time.

Too often, though, elapsed time influences a venture. If you have allocated $1 million toward a milestone in the fiscal year 1994, yet find that you've spent only $200,000 of it by November, you don't want to lose that money in 1995. There are some corporations that will let you allocate yet not spend the money in the same fiscal year. If, because you are waiting for a shipment of goods (for $800,000), you are unable to spend this money in 1994, some companies will say that you lose that money for 1994. And, it will impact on the budget you get for the following year. When you ask for $1.5 million, you may find that you receive only $300,000 based on your prior year's spending.

As a result of this syndrome, many individuals will spend the $800,000 in 1994 on almost anything so they don't lose the money in their next year's budget (actually they will hide the $800,000 they really need in 1995's budget). This creates great amounts of waste in an organization and something that can't occur in any economic time. Therefore, rather than be driven by Wall Street and corporate budgets, projects or ventures should be driven by needs when they occur. They should be opportunity driven. When an opportunity arises, financial resources should be ready to pounce. And budget games should not be a part of the venturing process.

ASSUMPTIONS: EXAMPLES OF THE MOST COMMON TYPES

COMPETITION ASSUMPTIONS

COMPETITION, COMPETITIVE ADVANTAGES, AND COMPETITIVE RESPONSE

The present and future competitors are The Lag Company and Zinc, Inc. They each have annual sales in excess of $10 million and can react quickly in terms of a change in price, service ability, and marketing strategy. Our competitive advantage is found in our patented proprietary technology.

FINANCIAL ASSUMPTIONS

Available Cash

We have $2 million available to finance the venture.

Cash Requirements

In order to fund this milestone, we need $7 million.

Gross and Net Margins

The expected gross and net margins of this venture are 45 percent and 15 percent, respectively.

Interest Rates

When we need to borrow funds, the interest rate we can expect to pay is 7.5 percent.

Investment Required to Meet P&L

The investment required to meet minimum profit and loss requirement is$3 million. Those items that require an investment to support them in the venture are property, plant, and equipment.

Time Requirements: P&L

The expected time required to reach the expected profit and loss statement projections is two years.

Time to Breakeven

The amount of time required to reach breakeven is four years.

MARKET ASSUMPTIONS

Definition

We define the market for our product/service in the following way: males, under 35 who earn at least $100,000 per year and drive sports cars.

Growth Rate

We expect the market to grow at the rate of 6 percent per year.

Product Demand

Our expected demand for the product in the market is 50,000 units in the first year, 75,000 in the second, and 100,000 thereafter.

Product Purchase Behavior

We expect the following product purchase behavior in the market: companies with 5 employees in cities of less than 100,000 people will purchase the product twice a year from their local distributor of office supplies. They will purchase 20 units at a time because they fundamentally believe the product will save them money. The person who will buy the product is a purchasing agent well versed in all of the competitive offerings.

Segmentation

We've segmented the market for our product to target upper-income college graduates because all market research shows that they are most likely to purchase it. Consumers in the Midwest enjoy our product more than do those in any other part of the country.

Size

The market size is 45 million units annually in the United States.

ORGANIZATIONAL ASSUMPTIONS

Available Team

The team available to participate in the venture is composed of one accountant with 10 years experience, a sales person who has sold to this industry for 15 years, and an office manager with no experience.

Management

In order to succeed, the firm needs a computer programmer who has knowledge of IDMS and can program in COBOL.

PRODUCT ASSUMPTIONS

Characteristics

The product is green, made of steel, and reinforced with a rubber plate. It costs $.30 per unit to produce. To achieve the needed quality (a variance of .33 millimeters), we have two quality control check points in the manufacturing process.

TECHNOLOGY ASSUMPTIONS

It Works

Fundamentally, the technology does work.

Development

The technology development costs are $5 million to create a prototype. We will need four industrial engineers for a period of two years, dedicated to development.

Production Capability

We are capable of producing the product or the service.

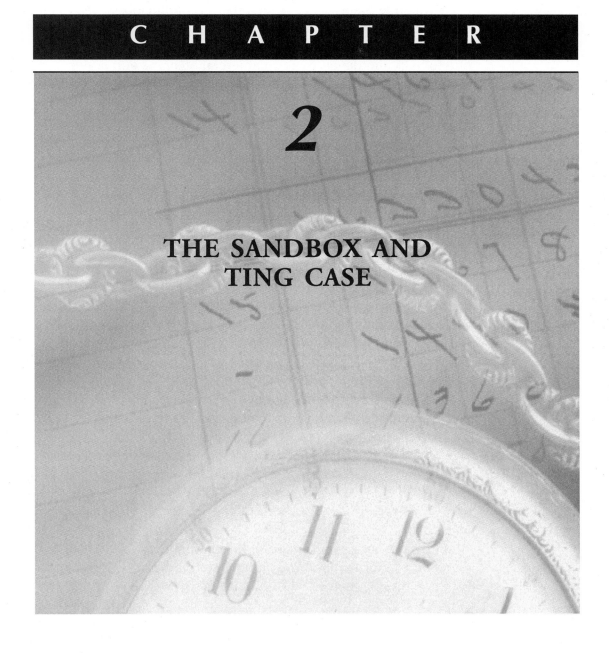

CHAPTER

2

THE SANDBOX AND TING CASE

Paul Sandbox graduated from the University of North Carolina with a degree in agricultural engineering and business. He loved plants. And he knew that he wanted to work with them. So he got a job watering plants. After several months on the job, while doing his route, Paul met an individual named Elroy Athens. Elroy owned a nursery called The North Carolina Nursery. Elroy needed someone to help him develop his commercial business and asked Paul if he would join the firm. Always looking for a way to better himself, Paul didn't hesitate to accept the job.

It was the summer of 1991 and Paul set out to develop the commercial side of the business for The North Carolina Nursery. Paul visited all of the businesses in Chapel Hill and the surrounding towns to drum up contracts. His mission was to sell plants to the local businesses and then service them. Servicing involved feeding, watering, and caring for the plants.

The service portion of the business was particularly appealing to Paul. He found that not every company wanted to buy a plant from him. Yet, it seemed as if every company had plants they didn't want to care for. The North Carolina Nursery benefited from Paul's salesmanship. Pretty soon he built the monthly maintenance to 46 clients ranging in size from $65 to $2,000 per month.

Everything looked rosy. Paul and Elroy got along famously. Paul realized, though, that Elroy just wasn't a good businessman. In fact, Paul found out that Elroy had purchased The North Carolina Nursery several years ago and had overpaid for it. He financed part of the purchase with a bank loan collateralized by his house. Most of the cash flow from the business was going toward the debt service on the purchase. While the business sold a fair number of plants, shrubs, and garden accessories, the margins weren't great enough to cover Elroy's debt service. Paul was Elroy's final hope. Paul had performed well but not well enough to cover all of Elroy's need for cash.

Elroy, desperate for anything, hired an entirely new management team to turn around The North Carolina Nursery. They lasted for three months before telling Elroy that it was time to fold the tent.

When Elroy decided that it was time to quit, he paid off all of his creditors and liquidated the business. Paul had hung in there until the end and Elroy told him to take all of the customers he had developed and start a new business. While Paul had never run a business by himself before, he felt that he could make a go of it, especially if he took The North Carolina Nursery's operation manager, Zach Ting, with him.

Paul immediately sent out letters to all 46 of the clients he had served with The North Carolina Nursery telling them that they would now be served by a new firm, Sandbox and Ting. Paul and Zach both had themselves laid off from The North Carolina Nursery and they both started to collect unemployment compensation. Zach borrowed $7,000 from an I.R.A., which they used to start the business. The North Carolina Nursery's bookkeeper, Kass Magilicutty, worked for free for about five months as they got the business off the ground.

Through the process, Paul and Zach didn't lose a single client. Yet they did lose a lot of their individual privacy. In order to save money, Paul and Zach decided to have the business operate out of the house into which they moved. Privacy for both was gone. The pair worked and lived together 24 hours a day. They even had to share a car because they had so little money.

The pair divided responsibilities in the company. Paul would continue in a marketing and sales role and assist with production when needed. Zach would ensure that the work got done. He scheduled the plant deliveries as well as the plant maintenance workers.

This setup worked. Paul and Zach felt as if all they did was work. Everything was going very well, so well that the pair decided to expand into the floral design business. They brought Thom McHeart on board to focus on this business. Thom was a one-man show. He'd sell business, design it, order the flowers, arrange them, and then deliver them.

During the 1992 Christmas season, Sandbox and Ting flourished. They did so well that people were lined up on the residential street where they operated to buy Christmas plants and flowers. Business was so good that they needed a large refrigerator for both the plants and flowers. To date, they had been keeping everything in an air-conditioned room, but there was no more room and a need to decrease the amount of spoilage. So, they bought a refrigerator and placed it outside of the house.

The neighbors began to complain. Not only was the refrigerator unsightly, but the lines of cars were a menace to the community. The community insisted that they move their business. On February 15, 1993, the entire company moved to an office building.

Now that the company moved, Paul and Zach got a little more privacy at home. It still wasn't enough for Paul, so he moved out. They felt good about the success they had achieved. Revenues hit almost $500,000 in 1992.

However, when Paul studied the financial statements, he observed that things might not be as rosy as he had originally thought. There were a lot of numbers that didn't really look right.

At the same time, Paul and Zach had some serious differences of opinion. Although each owned 50 percent of the business, each felt that the other wasn't doing enough. The two were so upset with one another that they hardly talked. Everyone in the company knew that something was going on.

Since Paul and Zach were so pivotal to the business, everyone in the company wanted them to resolve their disputes. Yet nothing seemed to work. As time went on, they became more upset with one another.

Additionally, Paul realized that they had never sat down and completed a formal business plan. Everything that had happened in the business so far was completely reactive. Now it was time to get serious about the business and do some planning. Zach didn't feel that this planning was necessary.

Paul wanted to understand just where the business was and, more important, where they should take it.

Questions

1. Imagine you are Paul. What are the most critical milestones that now face Sandbox and Ting?

2. Rate each milestone as go/no go, potential venture redirection, or low impact.

3. What are the underlying assumptions in each of the milestones?

CHAPTER

3

THE SPICE KITCHEN CASE (A)

On August 4, 1990, Anthony Rosinni was sitting in his Manhattan apartment reviewing his proposal for the acquisition of The Spice Kitchen. It was three o'clock in the afternoon. Anthony nervously awaited his final meeting with Carla Tortelli at five o'clock later that day. He had spent the past three months performing due diligence on The Spice Kitchen. He still had many questions with reference to its current operations and future potential. Anthony, 49, had started his career in the restaurant business. He was a manager for four years before being let go. He then went into the construction business, and for the next 18 years was a construction manager. With the help of his mother-in-law, he had just negotiated the last piece of financing. With Anthony's lifetime savings on the line, he was evaluating his proposal one last time. He was unsure about the accuracy of his valuation of the business.

COMPANY BACKGROUND

Nick and Carla Tortelli immigrated to Manhattan from Sicily in 1965. For the first four years, they worked in an Italian grocery store on West 6th and 4th Avenue. After learning about importing food products, and with the help of some friends, Nick and Carla decided to go into the spice business. With a small bank loan and personal savings, The Spice Kitchen began operations in 1969. They began as wholesale repackagers of olive oil. Slowly, as business prospered, they expanded their product line to include seasonings, flavorings, and other spices. In the late 70s, they opened a retail store next door to the warehouse distribution center.

The Spice Kitchen is currently owned and operated by Carla Tortelli in Little Italy, Manhattan. She inherited the business from her late husband Nick, after he passed away five years ago.

After five years of working alone, Carla was not interested in running the business and was actively soliciting proposals for its sale.

PRODUCT LINES

The Spice Kitchen in Little Italy is one of the largest importers, distributors, and retailers of spices and seasonings in the New York

City area. The Spice Kitchen has a very extensive and diversified product line that also includes extracts, sauce and gravy mixes, salad dressing, green olives, food coloring, coffee, tea, herbs, flavorings, and other specialty food products. The products, mainly retailed under The Spice Kitchen name, are targeted at price-conscious as well as bulk buyers. Spices from many countries around the world are shipped to the warehouse for processing. Spices are first cleaned and treated. Then, individual orders are packaged and shipped. All inventory is tracked by hand. When a particular spice is running out of stock in the retail store, the order is called in to the wholesale operation and filled immediately.

RETAIL OPERATIONS

The retail store, located at West 4th and 3rd Avenue is in the heart of Little Italy. The large sign and sandwich boards placed on 5th Street and 2nd Avenue give The Spice Kitchen excellent visibility. The Store was managed by the very capable Grace Magarelli, 43, who has lived in Little Italy all of her life. Her interpersonal skills and amiable personality make her an invaluable asset to the company. Her relationship with the customers and their high praise for the company keeps business steady. The store is open Monday through Friday from 6 A.M. to 5 P.M. and on Saturday from 9 to 12 A.M. In addition to Grace, there is one other full-time employee, Ed Teranova, and three part-time students from the area.

WHOLESALE OPERATIONS

Wholesale operations began in the late 70s. Nick decided to buy the retail store down the street from the retail warehouse. The office space is at the back of the warehouse. It is a very small area, with three offices, of approximately 1,500 square feet. Carla has her own office, while the other two offices are each shared by three vice presidents and the accountant. There are also two secretaries. The contents of the office, as well as those for the retail store and warehouse are listed in Exhibit 1 on page 39.

The warehouse is a two-story building, over 200,000 square feet. The inventory is trucked in and unloaded at the rear of the building. It is then forklifted to the designated production area. Getting to the second floor is very inconvenient—you have to walk up a ladder. The system of packaging is very random and disorganized. Raw sacks of produce are scattered all over the floor. There doesn't seem to be an area for quality control. The equipment is very old and out of date. Workers measure out quantities of spices and package them by hand. There is a significant amount of spices lying around, indicating possible spoilage and wastage.

SPICE INDUSTRY

Estimates put the total U.S. spice market at around $2 billion. The United States now supplies one-third of its total consumption from domestic suppliers. The remaining two-thirds come predominantly from Indonesia, India, and Madagascar. The principal port of entry for spice imports, accounting for approximately 50 percent of U.S. imports, is New York. Other significant ports include Los Angeles, San Francisco, and Baltimore. The major spice-growing areas in the United States are in California and New Mexico. The major spice-importing countries are China, Brazil, Turkey, Egypt, and some countries in Eastern Europe.

ECONOMIC

The consumption of spices in the United States hit a new record high in 1989, totaling more than 795,485,000 pounds. This represents a 50 million pound increase from 1988, according to the American Spice Trade Association. This increase is largely noticeable in hot spices. Domestic production as well as imports of red pepper increased by 14 million pounds while black and white peppers increased by 3.3 million pounds. The United States is the largest pepper-importing country and takes over 25 percent of worldwide production.

The past five years has seen an average consumption of 694 million pounds per year, with 561 million during the previous five years and a 451 million pound average for the five years before that.

During the 80s, production of fennel seed increased by 145 percent. Oregano increased 82 percent to 10.3 million pounds and basil increased 80 percent to 4 million pounds. Other spices that saw increases in consumption include black and white pepper, allspice, sesame seed, cumin seed, bay leaves, and thyme. While the market for spices started to grow after World War II, the last 15 years have seen the greatest increase.

SOCIAL TRENDS

There are several reasons for the increase in spice usage. First, higher demand for ethnic foods is increasing demand for spices. According to a director of the American Spice Trade Association, "Increasing demand for Mexican foods as well as for spaghetti sauces, salad dressings, barbecued products, seasoned snacks, and cajun foods are major factors in the demand increase for spices."

Another major factor is the trend toward a healthier diet. The trend toward using less salt in foods has resulted in a need to compensate for the flavor loss. Using spices as a substitute will continue in the future.

A relatively new spice type called the "oleoresin" continues to show strong demand. These extracts offer certain advantages over natural ground spices, such as consistency of quality, freedom from microorganisms, uniform dispersion in the product, and easy handling and storage. Rising import trends for both natural spices and oleoresins indicate that the increased use of oleoresins is not a replacement for natural spices, but is an expansionary effect of the demand for flavored food products.

CONSUMER ANALYSIS

The repackaged spice market can be segmented into high-quality spices and generic spices. Typically, a repackager will import spices from another country. He can either repackage them cheaply and sell them under a generic label, or reprocess and improve the product and sell it under a brand label. The repackagers have developed in-house cleaning and processing methods to remove bacteria and other unwanted materials from the raw product. Food service and industrial food manufacturers are the largest spice purchasers. They consume 60 percent of the total U.S. supply. This has been a 20 percent increase in the last 10 years.

HIGH QUALITY

Consumers are concerned with freshness and full-bodied flavors. Processors more carefully select, clean, and sterilize spices. Packaging is very important. New, clear, and shatter-resistant containers are usually demanded. Clear containers make inventory control easier. As well, an easy grip design prevents spilling or slipping, even with wet hands. Standard sizes are 7 inches high by 2 3/4 inches deep and 4 1/4 inches wide. A tamper-evident seal is mandatory and screw-caps with plastic closures are standard. This way, the essential oils and flavors are locked in for maximum freshness. Lastly, product content and proper usage on labels are provided to aid customers. The low-quality consumer does not demand all of the above characteristics. A lower price compensates for this difference.

COMPETITIVE ANALYSIS

The spice industry is very fragmented. With the exception of McCormicks, there are very few players with a national distribution base in the majority of states. Other notables include Durkee-French Foods and The Baltimore Spice Inc. The industry is thus more regional. In New York, for example, there are ten to twelve large wholesalers, who import product from different parts of the world, then repackage and label the new goods. On a wholesale level, competition comes from the ten to twelve large wholesalers. Specifically though, only 6 compete in the Italian district. On a retail level, competition comes from other retail stores of the six distributors. As well, it comes from small wholesalers supplied by other wholesalers and The Spice Kitchen.

MANAGEMENT

The firm consists of 7 employees in addition to Carla. Mickey Townsend has been the company's accountant since its founding. He is a personal friend of Nick. He handles all business affairs such as cash management, financing, dealings with banks, and legal counsel. John Satok is vice president of production. He is also in charge of purchasing raw materials. Paul Dal Bello is vice president of operations. In addition, his duties include new product research. The vice president in charge of marketing and public relations is Anna Foldes.

DISTRIBUTION/MARKETING

The Spice Kitchen has two channels of distribution: wholesale and retail. The wholesale division sells its product to large grocery stores (60 percent) and small distributors/wholesalers (40 percent). These small distributors/wholesalers in turn sell to small grocery stores, restaurants, and specialty food stores. The Spice Kitchen's products are also sold through their retail store, which sometimes competes with some of the small grocery stores and specialty food stores. In general, most of the retail stores sales are for home use.

Currently, The Spice Kitchen's main retail customers are Mexican and Italian. Mexican sales represent only a very small portion of total sales (5 percent), leaving them dependent on the Italian community. A growing market segment that seemed relatively untapped is the Indian community, which is notorious for its use of spices. Anthony wondered if it was possible to break into this market.

Several months ago, Anthony's mother-in-law went to a dinner party. There she was introduced to Carla, who casually mentioned that she was interested in selling the business. With Anthony's need to do something more entrepreneurial, he contacted Carla and his due diligence had begun. He had taken a tour of the plant and interviewed all of the employees. After learning more about the company, he became very interested and began serious discussions.

FINANCING

After the initial rounds of negotiations, an agreement was reached that if financing could not be in place by today, liquidated damages would amount to all cash payments, which were already placed in escrow.

Anthony had asked Carla for financial statements for the past two years. He also requested a projected income statement for 1990. Exhibits 2 through 7 (pages 41–46) have been provided by Mickey. Anthony believed that the proper way to value this business was to take the value of the buildings and add to it a multiple of retained earnings.

Value of buildings	$325,000		
Multiple of Retained Earnings	4 × 86,000	=	$344,000
			$669,000

The following shows Anthony's calculations for his perceived value of the different assets of the business and his method of financing.

	Perceived Value	Method of Financing
Machinery and Equipment	$50,000	$250,000
Cash Furniture and Fixtures	50,000	$94,000
PMM* Goodwill	44,000	$344,000
Inventory	100,000	
Non-Compete Agreement	100,000	
	$344,000	
Retail Store Building	$100,000	$25,000
Cash		$75,000
PMM*		$100,000

Warehouse	$225,000	$25,000
Cash		$200,000
PMM*		$225,000
Total Assets	$669,000	
Total Financing		$669,000

*PMM = Purchase Money Mortgage

Carla was willing to take $469,000 in the form of a Purchase Money Mortgage. Anthony was only able to get a $125,000 home equity loan. This left him $75,000 short. He felt that his last hope was his mother-in-law. She had agreed to take a $75,000 mortgage on her house. He promised her that she wouldn't lose her house and that this venture was a sure thing. She was currently evaluating the proposal.

Anthony had hired a lawyer, Winston David, who also specialized in taxation. Winston had tried to explain the advantages and disadvantages of different deal structures. Anthony was unsure whether he should buy the company or just the assets. As well, he wondered what form of ownership his company should adopt.

OTHER CONSIDERATIONS

During the previous three months, John Satok had been experimenting with the creation of a new spice. In partnership with a local food chemist, they had developed a potent spice, which did not seem to have any additives or chemicals that would cause health problems, such as ulcers. The trend toward health consciousness had not affected the industry yet, but it was only a matter of time before this became a consideration. The initial name for this product was "Hott Stuff." The product is still in the developmental stage, and it will probably be a year before it can be tested on the market.

A last consideration would be whether to sell the Habanero peppers fresh as whole peppers, like vegetables, or dried first, so that they can be preserved indefinitely. Further market research needed to be performed to answer these questions.

CONCLUSION

Because of the meeting with Carla in the afternoon, and all his cash payments to date as liquidated damages, Anthony began to worry. He had never been in the business of buying and selling companies and was unsure if he took the proper steps in his due diligence efforts.

He was very unskilled at finance and was confused by the complicated financing structure that Carla had proposed. In addition, he was not sure that the valuation method he used was appropriate in this case. He had bought a book on valuation, and followed the given example, a restaurant chain. He began to get very confused, as there were so many issues to deal with, internally as well as strategically. Anthony was wondering whether he had gone too far in an area in which he knew little.

Questions

1. What are the critical assumptions that need to hold for Anthony's valuation of the business?

2. What critical go/no go assumptions and major milestones must exist for The Spice Kitchen to succeed?

EXHIBIT 1   THE SPICE KITCHEN CASE (A)

OFFICE FURNISHINGS

Executive desk and credenza

Writing desk

Computer desk

Typing stand

4 Chairs

2 Wrought Iron Gates

2 Three-tier paper bins

Four-door lateral file cabinet

3 Two-door lateral file cabinets

2 Two-drawer file cabinets

Regulator wall clock

Keymaster wall mount box

8 Framed pictures

EQUIPMENT

AT&T Computer 6300 w/printer

Silver Reed EX42 typewriter

Westinghouse A/C 17500 BTU 9-81

Texas Instrument computer

Ademco alarm system

Telephone system (7 phones)

Savin 5020 copier

Panasonic stereo w/speaker

Sharp calculator

Panasonic pencil sharpener

2 Desk lamps

2 Rolodexes

RETAIL STORE

2 NCR cash registers

* 1 1/4 # Slicing scale

Tec SL 36-15L Dig scale

* #3 U.S. Slicing scale

Peanut butter maker

Emerson A/C

3 Franklin neck alarms

2 Scotch labelers

2 32-gallon steel cans w/lids

Assorted shelving

26 Wicker baskets

2-Tier shelf

Royal calculator

GLK phone system

2 Toledo 8430 dig scales

2 Ditting coffee grinders

Ceiling fan

Clock radio

2 Metco pricing guns

2 Tape dispensers

2 32-gallon plastic cans w/ lids

Wooden display counter

3-tier shelf

1980 Toyota supra (needs state inspection and clutch)

(continued)

EXHIBIT 1	**THE SPICE KITCHEN CASE (A)**

WAREHOUSE

EQUIPMENT & MACHINERY

Wilson MC 390 safe

One-floor electric conveyor

Westinghouse chest-type freezer

Sanyo microwave oven

2 Ceiling fans

Clamco sealing machine

Sears cement mixer

Hobart coffee grinder

Sears wet/dry vac.

Counter Boy tape dispenser

3 Floor fans

Three-tub S.S. sink

Steel shelving (heavy duty)

    6 Sections 5' x 8' x 8 h

    3 Sections 3.5 x 8 x 5 h

    3 Sections 8 x 8 x 2

Assorted wood shelving

Scales:

    Toledo 8431 digital

    Toledo 8213 digital

    Detecto 854 floor

    Toledo 861 floor

    Edlurid E 32 gram / oz

*4 Hand trucks (one needs a new wheel)

5'6" Movable stair

8' Conveyor rail

*Better pack tape dispenser

Two-floor electric conveyor

*GE Refrigerator (broken)

Bunn coffee maker

Cordery water cooler

Machine world sealer

Gibson cement mixer

*Bunn coffee grinder

2 Sears dehumidifiers

Airtemp air conditioner

3 Work tables

13 Plastic rectangular containers

Store-type display shelving

    6 Sections 4' x 6'

    14 Sections 3' x 6'

    16 Sections 4' x 5'

Entry foyer

4 Carts on wheels

6 Framed pictures

2 40" x 30" flat carts

2' 6" x 5' flat bed cart

2' x 4' flat bed cart

2 27" x 52" flat bed carts

2 10' conveyor rails

10 Rubbermaid 32 gallon containers w/ lids

*Needs replacing

EXHIBIT 2   THE SPICE KITCHEN CASE (A)

**MARISSA MEGAN LAW
CERTIFIED PUBLIC ACCOUNTANT
888 WEST 3RD AVENUE
NEW YORK, NY 10009**

The Spice Kitchen
34 West 4th Avenue
New York, NY
10089

Attention Mickey:

As per your request, I have compiled the accompanying Balance Sheet and the related Statement of Earnings for the years ended December 31, 1988, 1989, in accordance with standards established by the American Institute of Certified Public Accountants. A compilation is limited to presenting in the form of financial statements information that is the representation of Management. I have not audited or reviewed the accompanying financial statements and, accordingly, do not express an opinion or any other form of assurance on them.

The accompanying forecasted balance sheet and income statement for The Spice Kitchen, as of December 31, 1990, is Management's estimate of the most probable financial position and results of operations for the forecast period. Accordingly, the forecast reflects Management's judgment, based on present circumstances.

I have made a review of the financial forecast in accordance with applicable guidelines for a review of a financial forecast established by the American Institute of Certified Public Accountants. My review included procedures to evaluate both the assumptions used by Management and the preparation and presentation of the forecast. I have no responsibility to update this report for events and circumstances occurring after the date of this report.

Based on my review, I believe that the accompanying financial forecast is presented in conformity with applicable guidelines for presentation of a financial forecast established by the American Institute of Certified Public Accountants. I believe that the underlying assumptions provide a reasonable basis for Management's forecast. However, some assumptions inevitably will not materialize and unanticipated events and circumstances may occur; therefore, the actual results achieved during the forecast period will vary from the forecast, and the variations may be material.

Marissa Megan Law
Certified Public Accountant
New York, NY
June 27, 1990

EXHIBIT 3 **THE SPICE KITCHEN CASE (A)**

THE SPICE KITCHEN
Balance Sheet
For the Years Ending December 31, 1988, 1989
(Unaudited)

	1988	1989
Assets		
Current assets		
Cash	59,490	92,230
Accounts receivable	123,310	314,750
Inventory	813,190	909,690
Total current assets	995,990	1,316,670
Property and equipment		
Automobiles	189,310	189,310
Improvements	130,330	130,330
Furniture and fixtures	387,200	387,200
Total	706,840	706,840
Less accumulated depreciation	599,100	649,290
Net property and equipment	107,740	57,550
Total assets	1,103,730	1,374,220
Liabilities		
Current liabilities		
Accounts payable	290,970	83,210
Taxes payable (excluding income)	26,050	66,070
Accrued expenses	3,740	24,000
Accrued interest	44,800	62,800
Taxes payable (income)	42,750	31,320
Total current liabilities	408,310	267,400
Long-term debt		
Officer loan	216,540	196,540
Shareholders' equity		
Common stock	50,000	50,000
Retained earnings	428,880	860,280
Total shareholders' equity	478,880	910,280
Total liabilities and share-holders equities	1,103,730	1,374,220

EXHIBIT 4   THE SPICE KITCHEN CASE (A)

THE SPICE KITCHEN
Income Statement
For the Years Ending December 31, 1988, 1989, 1990E
(Unaudited)

	1988	1989	1990E
Sales	7,633,010	7,586,360	8,825,000
Cost of goods sold			
Inventory—beginning	609,000	813,190	909,690
Purchases	5,195,800	4,363,150	4,870,000
Direct labor	483,120	876,770	750,000
Freight - in	147,720	175,310	173,000
Payroll taxes—direct	51,980	96,900	83,000
Subtotal	6,487,620	6,325,320	6,785,690
Less ending inventory	813,190	909,690	1,077,010
Total cost of goods sold	5,674,430	5,415,630	5,708,680
Gross margin on sales	1,958,580	2,170,730	3,116,320
Operating expenses	1,753,900	1,673,210	1,789,000
Income before taxes	204,680	497,520	1,327,320
Less: taxes on income	45,500	66,120	435,000
Net income after taxes	159,180	431,400	892,320
Retained earnings—beginning	269,700	428,880	860,280
Retained earnings—end	428,880	860,280	1,752,600

EXHIBIT 5   THE SPICE KITCHEN CASE (A)

THE SPICE KITCHEN
Statement of Cash Flows
For the Years Ending December 31, 1988, 1989
(Unaudited)

Operating activities	1988	1989
Net income	159,180	431,400
Adjustments		
Depreciation	48,780	50,200
Changes in assets and liabilities:		
(Increase) decrease in:		
A/R and prepaid expenses	−66,390	−191,440
Inventory	−204,190	−96,500
Increase (decrease) in:		
A/P and accrued expenses	221,460	−169,510
Taxes payable	9,520	28,590
Net cash provided by operating activities	168,360	52,740
Investing activities		
Cash used : property and equipment	−42,460	0
Financing activities		
Proceeds from short- and long-term borrowings	0	300,000
Principal payments on short- and long-term borrowings	−115,350	−320,000
Net cash used in financing activities	−115,350	−20,000
Net increase (decrease) in cash	10,550	32,740
Cash and cash equivalents at beginning of year	48,940	59,490
Cash and cash equivalents at end of year	59,490	92,230

EXHIBIT 6   THE SPICE KITCHEN CASE (A)

THE SPICE KITCHEN
Schedule of Operating Expenses
For the Years Ending December 31, 1988, 1989, 1990E
(Unaudited)

	1988	1989	1990E
Advertising	47,430	90,860	90,000
Auto expense	5,450	11,250	11,000
Bank charges	3,930	2,540	2,500
Business gifts	500	0	0
Depreciation expense	48,780	50,200	200,200
Dues and subscriptions	2,990	1,290	1,300
Commissions	31,160	46,070	28,000
Contributions	700	2,000	2,000
Employee benefits	20,440	54,790	23,000
Insurance	221,760	126,340	125,000
Interest	20,720	22,500	325,000
Legal and accounting	86,200	129,300	29,000
Office expenses	46,490	34,820	34,000
Payroll—officers	318,000	312,000	300,000
Payroll—other	85,260	154,720	155,000
Payroll—taxes	43,390	51,580	50,000
Postage	6,870	9,200	9,000
Rent	306,900	288,000	144,000
Repairs	146,430	63,110	60,000
Miscellaneous taxes and licenses	84,890	52,540	50,000
Telephone	57,740	57,210	40,000
Travel allowance	46,120	0	0
Meals and entertainment	250	0	0
Utilities	121,100	112,890	110,000
Total operating expenses	1,753,500	1,673,210	1,789,000

EXHIBIT 7   THE SPICE KITCHEN CASE (A)

THE SPICE KITCHEN
Notes to Financial Statements
December 31, 1988, 1989 (Actual)
and December 31, 1990 (Forcasted)

Note 1—Summary of Significant Accounting Policies

Inventory

Inventory is stated at the lower of cost or market.

Property and Equipment

Property and equipment are stated at cost. Depreciation is calculated by the straight-line method and by the accelerated methods. Useful lives of the assets are as follows:

Automobiles	3–5 years
Improvements	5 years
Furniture and Fixtures	5–7 years
Buildings and Equipment	0–30 years

Depreciation on Buildings and Equipment was computed for the period 7/1–12/31/90. There is no salvage value.

Note 2—Interest was computed on loans of $650,000. at 10 percent interest for the period 7/1–12/31/89.

Note 3—Statement of Cash Flows

Additional disclosures required as part of the cash flows statement are as follows:

	1988	1989
Interest paid	$0	$92
Income taxes paid	$4,135	$1,094

C H A P T E R

4

THE SPICE KITCHEN CASE (B)

Mr. Anthony Rosinni, owner of The Spice Kitchen, was faced with some major strategic, financial, and operational decisions in the spring of 1993. A new product, Hott Stuff, had been very successful in test marketing and Anthony wondered about its potential. The margins on existing product lines were narrowing, and the threat of Durkee French, a large multinational spice company entering the market was imminent. With these problems in mind, Rosinni began to prepare a detailed plan to return to profitability, as three years of losses had continued to impede growth. In addition, he had overestimated the cash generation of the business and had overpaid by $250,000 for the business three years ago. This put a further unanticipated strain on resources. He knew that time was a factor, as competition was increasing and his financial position was deteriorating.

INDUSTRY UPDATE 1989–1993

The spice industry has been adversely affected by the recession. The industry has experienced an overall erosion in margins and ultimately earnings. Certain product lines have become unprofitable. Delinquencies in customer accounts have risen. Raw material costs have been rising. No matter how large the company, the spice market is very competitive. The major challenge today is to stop the dwindling number of customers as consolidations take place in the food industry. A loss of one customer is considered a major setback. Many small companies are merging to take advantage of synergies such as access to distribution channels and capital for investment. In the future, tighter margins, quality control, and innovation in marketing will be key factors for a competitive advantage.

The worldwide pepper market is expected to undergo a supply shock in the coming months. With major weather problems in India and Madagascar, the yield per acre of peppers is expected to fall dramatically. The cost of processing pepper will increase, thus driving up prices. Analysts predict a minimum jump of 25 percent within three weeks, which will raise havoc in the spice industry and cause spot shortages of some other spices. The Spice

Kitchen has already entered into fixed commitments for delivery of spices next month.

COMPANY UPDATE 1989–1993

Since Anthony bought The Spice Kitchen in 1989, the company has been in a continual state of decline. Anthony could not understand why the business, which was generating substantial free cash flow, was still having cash problems. He tried to personally analyze the business, without success. A main problem was the nature of the business, which operated primarily on a cash-only basis. Only recently have they sold on credit, to attract customers during the recession. As well, The Spice Kitchen's poor inventory management system made it difficult to keep track of production, inventory on hand, and sales. Through further investigation, Anthony discovered that the accountant had been committing fraud for quite some time. He had tricked Anthony into signing a power of attorney, by slipping it in with some other papers to sign. He had taken excess cash and invested in real estate deals. He had hoped to flip the properties quickly without anyone knowing and pocket the profit. However, the real estate market went sour and substantial losses resulted. These losses were what aroused Anthony's suspicions. He was uncertain of the action he should take. Carla still held a substantial interest in the company through the Purchase Money Mortgage. Now was not a good time to upset her, as one of Anthony's options was for her to take back the properties.

Lastly, there was a small disagreement (still unresolved) between Anna Foldes, vice president of marketing, and Grace Magarelli, manager of the retail store. The general argument was over transfer pricing. Traditionally, the wholesale operation sold spices to the retail store at cost. However, Anna now wanted to raise the price to that paid by other customers.

FINANCE

After the discovery of Mickey's fraudulent scheme, Anthony was unsure of the integrity of his current financials. Many of his projections for the future were based on historical results.

With all of the financial problems putting a strain on the business, a meeting had been set up with the Bank of New York. Ker Smith, an account manager who had dealt with The Spice Kitchen once in the past, was to meet with Anthony next week about possibly extending some form of financing. He wanted quarterly financial statements and monthly reports of inventory, receivables, and sales. Anthony needed to sit down with Mickey to go over the financials, as Anthony was not very good with the finances. Financial Statements are shown in Exhibits 1 through 3 on pages 54 through 56.

NEW PRODUCT DEVELOPMENT: HOTT STUFF

Over the past couple of years, a new spice has been under development. The new product, Hott Stuff, has just completed test marketing with very impressive figures. Production costs for Hott Stuff appear to be unusually low, resulting in margins as high as 150 percent. Cost of goods sold is running anywhere between $1.50–$1.60. Anthony felt that this would go down probably in the $1.35 to $1.45 range, as volume became greater and as current bottlenecks were removed. In addition, current production capacity for all lines combined is approximately 65 percent.

MARKETING

To begin with, Anthony was also wondering whether he should create a separate entity for Hott Stuff, or add it to The Spice Kitchen's existing product lines. The next consideration was his marketing strategy. The product could be introduced to a local food editor, who hopefully would give it a favorable review. He believed that to gain initial visibility, setting up point of sale displays in grocery stores as well as small food stores would be most effective. Coupons and other in-store promotions would follow. After a large population had sampled the product, hopefully word of mouth would have a positive impact. Hott Stuff was selling very well at $3.99 a jar, and there was a possibility that the market could bear a higher price. However, the point of unitary elasticity was unknown.

On Wednesday of last week, Naeem Advani, vice president of Steinberg's, came into the store. He was on vacation visiting some friends in New York. He was very impressed by Hott Stuff and is seriously considering putting the product in his chain of grocery stores across Canada. Exhibit 4 (page 57) shows some market share data for grocery stores in Ontario and throughout Canada.

ALTERNATIVES

With Carla still having a large interest in the company, she has kept a very close watch on the performance of the company. She knew that Anthony was in serious financial trouble. Although she had first lien on the properties and was not worried about her Purchase Money Mortgage, she did not want to see the business that her husband lived and died for go bankrupt. She had approached Anthony and offered to lessen his burden by taking back the buildings and leasing the properties to the company. A letter from her lawyer is shown in Exhibit 5 (page 58).

The deal is structured such that the original Purchase Money Mortgage is canceled. Under the new agreement, Anthony will sign a $155,000 promissory note, with the company's assets as collateral. The note bears a 5 percent interest charge and is being amortized as if it were a thirty-year term with a balloon payment and accrued interest due on October 1, 1997. Monthly payments of $832.09 shall be made commencing April 1, 1993, and the first day of each month thereafter.

The terms of the lease call for an initial five-year term, with rent on the retail store set at $265/month for the first 24 months and $425/month for the remaining 36 months. The warehouse will rent for $753/month for the first 24 months and $1,198/month for the remaining 36 months.

CORPORATE CAPABILITIES

During the past few months, Anthony had become very frustrated with himself and the business. Back in the spring of 1990, Anthony wanted a change after 18 years in the construction business. Since taking over The Spice Kitchen, the business has headed south, with no real sign of a turnaround. Not only is business poor, but there are many internal problems. Anthony was now working 80 to 90 hours a week with all of these problems. He started to wonder if this was really what he wanted. Now divorced, Anthony still hoped to remarry someday and settle down. He was so consumed by the business as of late, that he hadn't been out socially in almost nine months.

CORPORATE STRATEGY

Although margins in general had experienced a decline, some products still maintained high margins (above the industry average of 36–38 percent). There was a possibility that The Spice Kitchen could alter its product mix from its current level of 20 percent/80 percent high margin/low margin. However, there are many question marks associated with such a process, including production feasibility, switching costs, marketing, and competition. While the short-term costs may seem high, the long-term effects may make this strategy profitable.

OTHER CONSIDERATIONS

One of the major factors contributing to theft in the company stems from the poor inventory management system. There is none. Poor record keeping in conjunction with the lack of sales receipts due to the cash basis of the business have further exacerbated this problem. Paul Dal Bello, vice president of operations, has continued to pressure Anthony into modernizing with a computerized tracking system. This would allow for greater control over the business and result in greater efficiencies, especially in days of inventory. However, the downside would be in the cash business area.

CONCLUSIONS

Anthony was now faced with some tough choices, as profitability was dwindling. In addition to solving his immediate cash flow problems, Anthony began to ponder the long-term viability of the business. He felt that some sort of strategic plan needed to be developed. Some considerations included: shedding unprofitable businesses, repackaging the consumer spice line, trimming overhead, and lowering material costs. In addition, although Hott Stuff accounted for only 3 percent of total sales, Anthony believed that the potential was much greater if marketed properly. A future strategy needed to be developed.

However, Anthony had only a few thousand dollars, before having to seek other sources of funds. He was concerned about the financial resources needed to go forward with final development and marketing. With respect to internal issues, Anthony still had to deal with the theft and the poor inventory management system. Anthony's meeting with Ker Smith at the Bank of New York was fast approaching, and he didn't know if this option was better than dealing with Carla. So far the only alternative was the one that Carla proposed. Anthony wondered what other types of restructuring alternatives existed and how appropriate they would be at this time.

Questions

1. As a consultant to Anthony, what alternative courses of action do you foresee? Support your alternatives with a brief Income Statement and Balance Sheet along with a list of the assumptions you've made. What are your recommendations?

2. What are the risks and opportunities associated with the Hott Stuff opportunity? How do they translate into needed major and sub milestones?

EXHIBIT 1   THE SPICE KITCHEN CASE (B)

THE SPICE KITCHEN
Balance Sheet
For the Years Ending December 31, 1988–1992, 1993–1994E
(Unaudited)

	1988	1989	1990	1991	1992	1993E	1994E
Assets							
Current assets							
Cash	59,490	92,230	83,260	73,290	62,560	104,370	154,290
Accounts receivable	123,310	314,750	355,460	374,870	264,380	215,430	184,580
Inventory	813,190	909,690	891,496	829,091	771,055	848,161	1,017,793
Total current assets	995,990	1,316,670	1,330,216	1,277,251	1,097,995	1,167,961	1,356,663
Property and equipment							
Automobiles	189,310	189,310	189,310	189,310	189,310	189,310	189,310
Improvements	130,330	130,330	130,330	130,330	130,330	130,330	130,330
Furniture and fixtures	387,200	387,200	387,200	387,200	387,200	387,200	387,200
Total	706,840	706,840	706,840	706,840	706,840	706,840	706,840
Less accumulated depreciation	599,100	649,290	699,480	706,840	706,840	706,840	706,840
Net property and equipment	107,740	57,550	7,360	0	0	0	0
Total assets	1,103,730	1,374,220	1,337,576	1,277,251	1,097,995	1,167,961	1,356,663
Liabilities							
Current liabilities							
Accounts payable	290,970	83,210	97,640	145,320	136,340	169,840	167,830
Taxes payable (excluding income)	26,050	66,070	70,869	78,560	89,050	77,860	84,370
Accrued expenses	3,740	24,000	25,500	26,500	26,500	26,500	26,500
Accrued interest	44,800	62,800	65,000	75,890	76,340	86,900	85,970
Taxes payable (income)	42,750	31,320	35,640	37,860	43,760	50,700	51,340
Total current liabilities	408,310	267,400	294,649	364,130	371,990	411,800	416,010
Long-term debt							
Officer loan	216,540	196,540	196,540	108,532	268,834	697,618	1,102,066
Shareholders' equity							
Common stock	50,000	50,000	50,000	50,000	50,000	50,000	50,000
Retained earnings	428,880	860,280	884,395	594,287	−21,613	−395,905	−212,689
Total shareholders' equity	478,880	910,280	934,395	644,287	28,387	−345,905	−162,689
Total liabilities and shareholders' equity	1,103,730	1,374,220	1,337,576	1,277,251	1,097,995	1,167,961	1,356,663

EXHIBIT 2   THE SPICE KITCHEN (CASE B)

THE SPICE KITCHEN
Income Statement
For the Years Ending December 31, 1988–1992, 1993–1994E
(Unaudited)

	1988	1989	1990	1991	1992	1993E	1994E
Sales	7,633,010	7,586,360	7,434,633	6,914,209	6,430,214	7,073,235	8,487,882
Cost of goods sold							
Inventory—beginning	609,000	813,190	796,926	741,141	689,261	758,188	909,825
Purchases	5,195,800	4,363,150	4,275,887	4,233,128	4,190,797	4,400,337	4,840,370
Direct labor	483,120	876,770	885,538	894,393	903,337	948,504	1,043,354
Freight - in	147,720	175,310	171,804	159,778	148,593	163,452	196,143
Payroll taxes—direct	51,980	96,900	97,869	98,848	99,836	104,828	115,311
Subtotal	6,487,620	6,325,320	6,228,024	6,127,288	6,031,825	6,375,309	7,105,003
Less ending inventory	813,190	909,690	891,496	829,091	771,055	848,161	1,017,793
Total cost of goods sold	5,674,430	5,415,630	5,336,528	5,298,196	5,260,770	5,527,148	6,087,211
Gross margin on sales	1,958,580	2,170,730	2,098,105	1,616,012	1,169,444	1,546,087	2,400,672
Operating expenses	1,753,900	1,673,210	1,638,990	1,471,120	1,350,345	1,485,379	1,782,455
Income before taxes	204,680	497,520	459,115	144,892	−180,901	60,708	618,216
Less: taxes on income	45,500	66,120	435,000	435,000	435,000	435,000	435,000
Net income after taxes	159,180	431,400	24,115	−290,108	−615,901	−374,292	183,216
Retained earnings—beginning	269,700	428,880	860,280	884,395	594,287	−21,613	−395,905
Retained earnings—end	428,880	860,280	884,395	594,287	−21,613	−395,905	−212,689

EXHIBIT 3   THE SPICE KITCHEN CASE (B)

THE SPICE KITCHEN
Ratio Analysis
For the Years Ending 1988–1992, 1993–1994E

Profitability	1988	1989	1990	1991	1992	1993E	1994E
Sales	7,633,010	7,586,360	7,434,633	6,914,209	6,430,214	7,073,235	8,487,882
Cost of goods sold							
Inventory—beginning	8%	11%	11%	11%	11%	11%	11%
Purchases	68%	58%	58%	61%	65%	62%	57%
Direct labor	6%	12%	12%	13%	14%	13%	12%
Freight - in	2%	2%	2%	2%	2%	2%	2%
Payroll taxes—direct	1%	1%	1%	1%	2%	1%	1%
Subtotal	85%	84%	84%	88%	94%	89%	83%
Less Ending Inventory	11%	12%	12%	12%	12%	12%	12%
Total Cost of Goods Sold	74%	72%	72%	76%	82%	77%	71%
Gross margin on sales	26%	29%	28%	23%	18%	22%	28%
Operating expenses	23%	22%	22%	21%	21%	21%	21%
Income before taxes	3%	7%	6%	2%	–3%	1%	7%
						0%	0%
Less: taxes on income	1%	1%	6%	6%	7%	6%	5%
						0%	0%
Net income after taxes	2%	6%	0%	–4%	–10%	–5%	2%
Stability							
Net worth to total assets	0.43	0.66	0.70	0.50	0.03	–0.30	–0.12
Liquidity							
Current ratio	2.44	4.92	4.51	3.51	2.95	2.84	3.26
Acid test	0.45	1.52	1.49	1.23	0.88	0.78	0.81
Working capital	587,680	1,049,270	1,035,567	913,121	726,005	756,161	940,653
Efficiency							
Age of receivables (days)	10.00	10.00	13.00	65.00	67.00	50.00	30.00
Age of payables	4.00	4.00	15.00	15.00	30.00	30.00	10.00
Net fixed assets/sales	0.01	0.01	0.00	0.00	0.00	0.00	0.00

EXHIBIT 4   **THE SPICE KITCHEN CASE (B)**

THE SPICE KITCHEN:
MARKET PROFILE OF SELECTED
CANADIAN SUPERMARKET CHAINS

RETAIL SUPERMARKET	CANADIAN MARKET SHARE	ONTARIO OUTLETS
Loblaws Companies	17%	135
Steinberg (includes Miracle Food Mart)	15	104
Provigo	3	Not Available
Safeway	10	26
A & P	0	114
Dominion	8	219
Food City	5	47

Source: *Business Canada,* Spring 1991.

EXHIBIT 5 **THE SPICE KITCHEN CASE (B)**

WU GOLDSTEIN GREENSPAN AND HUKKAWALA
Attorneys at Law
85 West 42nd Street
New York, NY 10027

December 12, 1992

Winston David, Esquire
CHANG & DAVID
27 East 39th Street
New York, NY 10069

Dear Winston:

Enclosed are the Promissory Note, Security Agreement, and Lease with blacklined revisions that clarify the agreement we negotiated.

The only addition I made was to add mutual general releases to the Security Agreement. This is consistent with our numerous discussions that the enclosed documents supersede all prior obligations of the parties, one to the other.

Carla continues to be concerned about deferred maintenance on both of the buildings. She is particularly concerned about animal and/or bird infestation. One of the reasons she was willing to agree to this restructuring is that she believed that the reduced monthly obligation would enable Anthony to maintain the buildings properly. He has been living with the reduced monthly obligation for six months now and should be addressing some of the deferred maintenance.

Anthony has said that he will not be responsible to Carla for the existing Code Enforcement Citation. The agreement between the parties is that neither shall have the right to compel the other to correct the problem with the basement walls. I have assumed that it is also understood that neither shall have the right to defend a governmental enforcement action by saying that it is the other's responsibility.

Paragraph 8 (c) of the printed Lease should not be deleted. If there are governmental requirements or citations with regard to the occupancy of the premises, they should be the tenant's responsibility.

In reviewing the Promissory Note, the second sentence of the second paragraph on the first page is less than clear. Perhaps it would be better to attach an amortization schedule and net down the balance due to reflect credits for the payments that have been made on account.

Please review these documents and let me know whether they are ready for execution.

Very Truly Yours,

Richard L. Greenspan

RLG:dms
Enclosures
cc: Carla Tortelli (w/enc.)

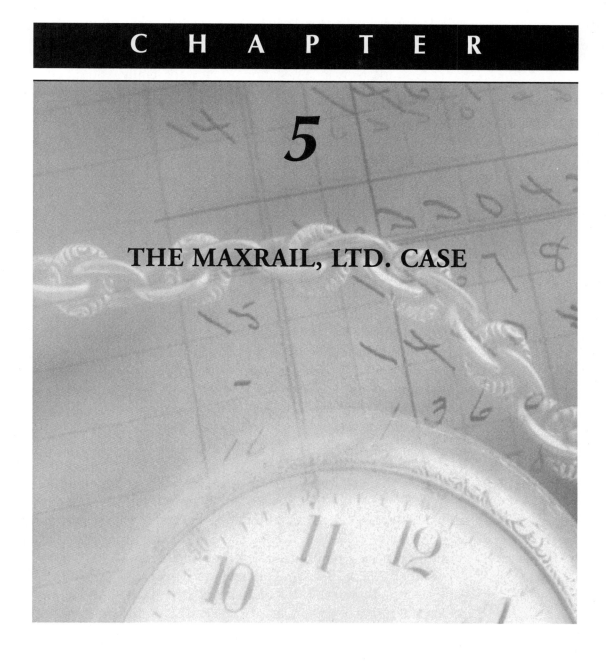

CHAPTER

5

THE MAXRAIL, LTD. CASE

It was May 1992. Summer was just settling into the eastern United States. Emily was commuting to her job in New York City from her home in Bucks County, Pennsylvania. She arose every morning about 6:00 A.M., drove her car to the Trenton, New Jersey, train station and waited there for either an Amtrak or New Jersey Transit commuter train. At approximately 7:00 A.M., she would board a train to the Newark, New Jersey, station. At Newark, Emily would transfer to the PATH train, a local train that transports riders to the World Trade Center in New York. In New York, she'd walk across the street to her position as an executive in a bank.

In the evening, Emily would reverse her direction and head home. Frequently, when she reached Newark, New Jersey, she would find the commuter train packed with people, like sardines in a can. No big deal, you say, unless you do it every day, pregnant.

Emily found that many of the passengers completely ignored the fact that she was pregnant. They left her standing through much of the journey back to Trenton. As months passed, Emily grew tired of the commute but realized that she couldn't just quit her well-paying job at the bank in New York.

One day, Emily's husband, Sam, rode the train with her. He was appalled by the fact that Emily was forced to stand in the train. Sam was so disturbed that he asked the conductor if Amtrak could put more cars on the commuter trains. The conductor told Sam that funds for new railroad cars came through the appropriations given to Amtrak by Congress. He did let Sam know about a special "club" car called the Princeton Club, which transported commuters to New York from Princeton.

Sam didn't want his wife riding to and from New York in discomfort. So he called the Amtrak office in Washington and asked them either to put more railroad cars in service on the commuter trains in what is known as "the corridor" (the northeast corridor of train service between Washington, D.C., and Boston) or to have Amtrak create a "Trenton Club" to run from Trenton.

Somehow, Sam was directed to the vice president of sales of Amtrak, John Bancroft. Mr. Bancroft told Sam that he couldn't put additional railroad cars in service. He told Sam that he was free to put his own car in service between Philadelphia and New York, on a daily basis. Now what should Sam do?

Sam realized that it was time to seize the entrepreneurial initiative. He called an old friend of his from business school, Henry Nop. Henry had taken a job when he graduated from school with Conrail (a large freight operation in the United States). And Sam knew that Henry had been a passenger and freight rail enthusiast from way back. Sam recalled that Henry had ridden the passenger rails in most of the continents throughout the globe. He told Henry that he wanted to buy a passenger railroad car but he didn't tell him the complete reason. You see, Sam was concerned that Henry would think the idea was so good that he might do it himself.

Henry's initial reaction was amazement. He couldn't believe that Sam had accumulated enough money to contemplate purchasing a railroad car. As Sam heard Henry, Sam began to wonder just how much this undertaking was going to cost him. Henry gave Sam the name of a gentlemen in Philadelphia (Benjamin Nevil) who was restoring old railroad cars. Henry was sure that Benjamin could help Sam locate a railroad car.

Sam called Benjamin and they set up a meeting at Benjamin's very own railroad terminal, near Philadelphia's main railroad station. Sam couldn't believe his eyes as he walked into the terminal. When he opened the door, three fully enclosed railroad sidings were in sight. And on them were all types of railroad cars, locomotives, and cabooses. Model trains were nothing. This represented the rich man's full gauge play toy.

Benjamin and Sam took an immediate liking to one another. Even though it was a cold winter day and the terminal wasn't heated, they talked for hours about the idea of running a commuter service between Philadelphia and New York. Benjamin's son, Evan Nevil, quickly identified some passenger cars that might be able to be purchased and restored; they were sitting idle in an Amtrak yard. Benjamin volunteered Evan to inspect the cars and file a full engineering report to Sam, all at a minimal charge.

Sam realized that he had reached a milestone in what was now becoming a venture. And he told Evan to proceed with his pursuit of a railroad car.

Meanwhile, Sam went back to John Bancroft, the vice president of sales of Amtrak and began to negotiate a contract for service. Amtrak offered Sam a ten-year contract for a commuter train between Philadelphia and New York. The contract specified a

$1.10 mileage charge for the 90-mile journey between Philadelphia and New York. It had a $300 per month parking fee for leaving the car at Philadelphia's 30th Street Station and New York's Pennsylvania Station. And it specified that the railroad car have $10 million of liability insurance.

Sam had become quite friendly with Benjamin by this time. Benjamin offered to help Sam in any way that he could with this pursuit. Benjamin introduced Sam to an Amtrak employee who showed an interest in running the day-to-day operations of the service. He also volunteered to help Sam restore any railroad car that they might find, at a reasonable rate.

On November 22, 1992, Sam and Emily's son, Max, was born. While, at one level, it seemed no longer necessary to travel down the rails to make this venture work, it became an obsession with Sam. He liked the idea of a low technology business with repeat revenues. So, on January 1, 1993, in a single day, as a new year's resolution, Sam sat down and wrote a draft business plan for a railroad line he named after his son, Max—MaxRail, Ltd.

DRAFT

BUSINESS PLAN

MaxRail, Ltd.

1 JANUARY 1993

TABLE OF CONTENTS

I. Executive Summary

    A. Background

II. The Business

    A. The Market

        1. Target Market

        2. Market Size

        3. Market Growth

        4. Competition

        5. Comparative Advantages over Competition

    B. The Operation

        1. Operational Description

            a. Transportation

            b. Food Service

            c. Cellular Telephone Service

            d. Charter Service

            e. Amenities

    C. Financial Information

        1. Sources and Uses Statement

        2. Profit and Loss Statements (Three-Year Summary)

        3. Profit and Loss Statement Assumptions

        4. Cash Flow Statement (One-Year Summary)

        5. Cash Flow Statement Assumptions

    D. Exhibit

    Exhibit A: Market Research

EXECUTIVE SUMMARY

The MaxRail line has been established to carry commuters, roundtrip, from Philadelphia (and points in between) to New York City. With the increased growth of people living in this corridor, commuters are forced to ride the train standing from their departure to their arrival, because the United States Congress will not appropriate more money for the purchase of additional capital equipment (i.e., railcars).

The MaxRail line will, initially, place one railcar on the back of one scheduled Amtrak train (Clocker 202, North and Clocker 225, South) each working day of the year.

The MaxRail line will position itself as a luxury travel alternative to the normally cramped and "less than homey" conditions found in Amtrak travel. MaxRail commuters cannot help but be more productive during their business day if they do not have to endure the crowding, herding, and jagged nerves characteristic of the usual journey.

A limited partnership is being formed to fund the acquisition and restoration of the first railcar on the MaxRail line. The partnership seeks $150,000. Each share, priced at $10,000, will give the investor a 20 percent return on investment, except for the first year when that return will be only 10 percent. Each limited partner will also get his pro rata share of the depreciation on the railcar (1/15 per share). Finally, each limited partner will have use of the railcar for one weekend each year. The limited partner will pay for additional insurance, running rail rates, and any attendant services necessary for his travel during that weekend.

BACKGROUND

The MaxRail line was born out of anger. The general partner's wife was commuting to New York from Trenton, New Jersey. Her journey would take her to Newark, New Jersey, at which point she would board the PATH train to the World Trade Center in New York. Every evening she would reverse this course to get home. Almost every day, on the trip home, as she boarded at Newark, New Jersey, she would find herself standing until she got to Trenton, New Jersey. She was pregnant.

The general partner made this trip with his wife and would constantly have to intimidate someone into giving his wife a seat. When the general partner asked an Amtrak conductor why there were not more railcars on the trains, the conductor referred him to the United States Congress for an appropriation. This same conductor, though, told him about an "exclusive occupancy" car that ran between Princeton and New York every day. The general partner decided to have Amtrak start such a service between Trenton and New York for his wife. Amtrak offices in both Washington and New York City felt it was an idea with merit yet did not have the railcar or the appropriation to add one onto this route.

When questioned as to alternatives, Amtrak said that the general partner could buy a railcar and place it in service on the back of the regular Amtrak commuter service. After speaking with many railroad buffs and Amtrak officials, the general partner saw that this idea not only had merit, but also had a profitable bottom line, if operated as a business.

THE BUSINESS

The MaxRail line will provide luxury rail service for the commuter. Its first car will serve the Philadelphia to New York (and points in between) commuter. The idea is to create a pleasurable experience for the commuter who is forced to travel sometimes three hours per day.

There is proven demand for the service as Amtrak used to run a parlor car service between Philadelphia and New York every day. It was always sold out. It was only during the Amtrak reorganization, which made Passenger Services the stepchild to Freight, that such service was discontinued because it was considered "elitist."

THE MARKET

The target market is the commuter who travels from Philadelphia (or points north) to and from New York City, every workday. The target market is also those persons who have a fairly predictable work schedule as the MaxRail line will initially be traveling on only one train to New York every day (Clocker 202) and one train from New York every day (Clocker 225).

The market size is best determined with a statistic given out by the stationmaster at Trenton, New Jersey. Ten years ago, 3,000 people every month traveled to New York City from Trenton. Today, 3,000 people travel that route every day. In fact, a new parking lot was constructed several years ago at the Trenton train station. The day after it opened, it was filled. This market growth is found also in Princeton, New Jersey, where about half the commuters must stand on the train in the morning and never get a parking space at the Princeton train station.

Property values in this corridor are still inexpensive vis-a-vis Connecticut and New York City. Therefore, more people are moving into the corridor. The commuter crowding is getting worse every day. (This commuter congestion is also a problem on the major roadways.)

It appears that growth will continue in this market, yet Amtrak and New Jersey Transit have put no new railcars into service due to lack of capital appropriations.

Direct competition for the MaxRail line is Amtrak and New Jersey Transit. It is highly unlikely that the severe shortage of equipment will be remedied soon, unless there is some grand political movement to do so. Additionally, it is unlikely that service standards on each of these lines will change dramatically, unless they are privatized (another unlikely situation). Finally, it is unlikely that Amtrak or New Jersey Transit will offer luxury service that directly competes with the MaxRail line as they are not run by profit-minded executives, but rather government, civil service-minded individuals.

The advantage of the MaxRail line over Amtrak and New Jersey Transit will be high-quality service. MaxRail line's greatest comparative advantage will be its customer service.

THE OPERATION

Transportation

Initially, the MaxRail line's first railcar will travel between Philadelphia and New York City, roundtrip, every day. It is expected that this car will be a restored New York Central 1947 Budd stainless steel car. The railcar will travel on the back of the Clocker 202 train, which leaves Philadelphia every morning at 6:20 A.M. It travels the following route:

Clocker 202	**Station**	**Time**
	Philadelphia	6:20 A.M.
	North Philadelphia	6:30
	Trenton	6:58
	Princeton Junction	7:10
	New Brunswick	7:26
	Newark	7:51
	New York	8:08

On its return trip, the railcar will travel on the back of the Clocker 225 train, which leaves New York City every evening at 6:05 P.M. It travels the following route:

Clocker 225	**Station**	**Time**
	New York	6:05 P.M.
	Newark	6:23
	Princeton Junction	6:57
	Trenton	7:11
	North Philadelphia	7:38
	Philadelphia	7:48

Every evening, the railcar will be parked in 30th Street Station, Philadelphia, waiting to be placed on Clocker 202 the next morning. Throughout the morning and the afternoon, the railcar will be parked in Penn Station, New York, waiting to be placed on Clocker 225 that evening.

The Food Service

This service will be contracted out. Bids will be solicited from several restaurants and food service vendors. These establishments include The Yardley Inn, Yardley, Pennsylvania; Marvin Gardens, New York City; and, ARA Food Services. Before the vendor is selected, MaxRail will carefully evaluate the operator's experience and quality in providing first-class service for the MaxRail line.

These organizations will serve breakfast on the journey to New York on Clocker 202 and snacks and drinks and light dinner on the journey from New York City to Philadelphia on Clocker 225.

The food service operation will also be responsible for keeping the railcar spotlessly clean. It is anticipated that MaxRail will command $10,000 per year for this concession.

Cellular Telephone Service

There will be two portable cellular telephones on board, initially. Projections assume a utilization of 50 percent for the three-hour train ride. The anticipated revenue figure also assumes that $.20 per minute can be achieved as the margin for offering the service.

Charter Service

Each of the limited partners will be entitled to use the railcar for one weekend per year. This use leaves 37 available weekends for charter of the car. It is assumed that the car will be chartered only 2 1/2 of these weekends (5 days) each year. The limited partners or the chartering party will be responsible for additional insurance, running rail rates, and any attendant services necessary for this weekend travel. Thus, no additional costs will be incurred to the MaxRail line.

Amenities—The 1947 Budd Railcar

The specific car available for purchase is former New York Central coach, number 2921. The car has had all the coach seats removed. Improvements that have been made to the car include 480 volt Head End Power (HEP) to upgrade to Amtrak 1991 standards; 110 volt interior lighting; Mar-Guard windows in Bronze (AAR 223 approved); overhead heat with two-stage floor heat, all electric; renewed interior window frames; new A.C. motors on most of the 480 volt system; 27 pin pass through, one side; Amtrak approved car mounted marker lights, both ends; water tank wrapped with electric heat protection with thermostat; brake cylinders converted to 7 1/2 inch compo brake shoes; new plumbing inside car; all new electrical locker for HEP and interior lighting; battery charger and a set of Ni-Cad batteries. The car has roller bearings and tight-lock couplers and an all stainless steel body construction.

The car will have a completely new floor plan. Design work for the plan will be performed by J M & Associates, historic preservation architects. Implementation of the design will be managed and performed by Benjamin Nivel, who is presently overseeing the restoration of many railroad cars.

Appointments for the car will resemble that of a five-star restaurant or a world class hotel—mahogany paneling; oriental carpeting; paintings on the walls; attendants in white uniforms with brass buttons. Further additions will be made as budget permits. The goal is to recreate an atmosphere of quality and gentility in which travel becomes a pleasurable experience.

Source and Uses of Funds

Sources

Limited Partnership Offering	$150,000
Total Sources	$150,000

Uses

Purchase of New York Central coach, number 2921	$ 38,000
Legal and accounting expenditures associated with the offering	$ 7,000
Restoration of railcar	$ 70,000
Initial operating expenses outlay (i.e., printing, advertising, telephone)	$ 5,000
Reserve fund	$ 30,000
Total uses	$150,000

MaxRail Line
Projected Profit and Loss Statement (with Limited Partnership)
Year 1 (Selling Food Concession)
($500 Annual Subscription/Normal Commuter Rate)

Annual revenues	40 Seats Phila-NYC	45 Seats Phila-NYC	50 Seats Phila-NYC	56 Seats Phila-NYC
Annual subscriptions	$ 20,000.00	$ 22,500.00	$ 25,000.00	$ 28,000.00
Annual fees	74,400.00	83,700.00	93,000.00	104,160.00
Food concession	10,000.00	10,000.00	10,000.00	10,000.00
Cellular telephone	9,360.00	9,360.00	9,360.00	9,360.00
Interest income	3,000.00	3,000.00	3,000.00	3,000.00
Other income	5,000.00	5,000.00	5,000.00	5,000.00
Total revenues	121,760.00	133,560.00	145,360.00	159,520.0
Expenses				
Insurance	$ 18,264.00	$ 20,034.00	$ 21,804.00	$ 23,928.00
Maintenance	6,000.00	12,000.00	12,000.00	12,000.00
Parking	1,800.00	3,600.00	3,600.00	3,600.00
Debt service	0.00	0.00	0.00	0.00
Mileage @$1.10/mile	25,049.00	25,049.00	25,049.00	25,049.00
Miscellaneous	12,000.00	12,000.00	12,000.00	12,000.00
Total expenses	63,113.00	72,683.00	74,453.00	76,577.00
Net income before distribution and depreciation	$ 58,647.00	$ 60,877.00	$ 70,907.00	$ 82,943.00
Partnership distribution ($150,000 x .2)	$ 30,000.00	$ 30,000.00	$ 30,000.00	$ 30,000.00
Net income before taxes	$ 28,647.00	$ 30,877.00	$ 40,907.00	$ 52,943.00

ASSUMPTIONS TO MAXRAIL PROFIT AND LOSS STATEMENT

1. The Profit and Loss Statement is cast on an annual basis.

2. Revenues consist of several components:

    a. Subscription fees. These subscription fees are payable, annually, at the commencement of service. The subscription fee is $500 per year.

    b. Annual fees. These fees represent a monthly fee for riding the rails on an ongoing basis. This fee is payable in advance of service.

    c. Food concession. The food concession will be contracted out. Bids for the service will be accepted and the one bid meeting the highest quality of service standards will be chosen. It is assumed that the successful bidder will pay $10,000 per year for the right to operate this concession.

    d. Cellular telephone. There will be two portable cellular telephones on board, initially. These projections assume a utilization of 50 percent for the three-hour train ride. This revenue figure also assumes that $.20 per minute can be achieved as the margin for offering the service.

    e. Interest. The contingency fund of $30,000 is expected to generate $3,000 income each year.

    f. Other income. On a limited basis, the railcar will be chartered out on weekends. It is assumed that the railcar will be chartered out five weekend days during the course of the year for $1,000 per day. During these charters, the chartering party will bear all variable expenses (i.e., running rail mileage, insurance, and attendant).

    g. Due to the uncertainty as to the type of train car that will finally be put into service, calculations have been made for passenger seating of 40, 45, 50, and 56 in the car. The car under most serious consideration, a Budd 1947 Coach, originally had 56 seats in it.

    h. The first year revenues reflect the fact that the railcar will not be in service for the first six months while it is being restored.

3. Expenses consist of the following:

a. Insurance. The Daniel and Henry Company, insurers of AAPRCO (American Association of Private Rail Car Owners), verbally quoted a premium of 15 percent of gross receipts as the premium for $5 million liability (the place where Amtrak's coverage becomes relevant). Their blanket AAPRCO policy shows premiums for this coverage as only $5,475 per year. The company said it would have to evaluate Amtrak's liability limits vis-a-vis the Rail Tariff before it could definitively give a price quote. The premium will not exceed the 15 percent of gross receipts, though. The premium will include business interruption insurance. In case of mechanical difficulty, passengers will be placed on a normal car in the Amtrak fleet and their fares will be underwritten by MaxRail. This business interruption insurance will cover this contingency.

b. Maintenance. This figure is based on a complete restoration of the railcar and putting it into service in such condition. The President of the Pennsylvania Historical Rail Association states that this $1,000 figure is a high estimate of actual costs.

c. Parking. This figure represents the price that the vice president of Amtrak has quoted to MaxRail. It covers daily parking in New York City's Penn Station and Philadelphia's 30th Street Station. Amtrak will contractually bind themselves to this price for a 10-year period. The contract is presently being drafted in the Amtrak legal department.

d. Debt service. Using the limited partnership vehicle, there is no debt service.

e. Mileage. This $1.10 per rail mile represents the price that the vice president of Amtrak has quoted to MaxRail. It covers the daily roundtrip to New York City from Philadelphia. It was calculated with the assumption that the car would run every weekday of the year. This number is therefore high as holidays are not taken into account.

f. Miscellaneous. A miscellaneous category of $1,000 per month is slated to cover telephone, mailings, accounting, legal, and miscellaneous expenses.

4. Partnership distribution. It is assumed that $150,000 is to be raised through the limited partnership offering. Railcar pur-

chase, restoration, and legal and accounting expenses are to be paid from this amount. Additionally, a contingency fund of $30,000 is to be set up from this pool. Annual distribution of 20 percent is anticipated to be the ongoing return for the limited partners. The depreciation of the railcar will also be passed on to the limited and general partners of the partnership.

5. Net income before taxes will be distributed to the General Partner as a management fee.

MaxRail, Ltd. : Cash Flow Statement

Year 1

	Month 1	Month 2	Month 3	Month 4	Month 5	Month 6
Beginning cash balance	$ 0.00	$106,250.00	$87,125.00	$67,833.33	$48,375.00	$33,778.13
Investment	150,000.00	0.00	0.00	0.00	0.00	0.00
Cash receipts	1,250.00	875.00	708.33	541.67	403.13	46,450.00
Total available cash	151,250.00	107,125.00	87,833.33	68,375.00	48,778.13	80,228.13
Cash expenditures	45,000.00	20,000.00	20,000.00	20,000.00	15,000.00	9,258.08
Ending cash balance	106,250.00	87,125.00	67,833.33	48,375.00	33,778.13	70,970.05

Year 1

	Month 7	Month 8	Month 9	Month 10	Month 11	Month 12
Beginning cash balance	$70,970.05	$77,700.06	$84,236.15	$90,743.37	$97,304.82	$103,837.62
Investment	0.00	0.00	0.00	0.00	0.00	0.00
Cash receipts	15,738.09	15,794.17	15,765.30	15,819.53	394.21	531.98
Total available cash	86,708.14	93,494.23	100,001.45	106,562.90	97,699.03	104,369.60
Cash expenditures	9,258.08	9,258.08	9,258.08	9,258.08	9,258.08	9,258.08
Ending cash balance	77,450.06	84,236.15	90,743.37	97,304.82	88,440.95	95,111.52

ASSUMPTION TO CASH FLOW STATEMENTS

1. Beginning cash in Month 1 is presumed to be zero.
2. In Month 1, the limited partnership offering is expected to raise $150,000 for use by MaxRail.
3. Cash receipts in Month 1 are presumed to be interest income on the principal of $150,000.
4. Cash expenditures in Month 1 are the purchase of the railcar ($38,000) plus legal expenditures and other items associated with the purchase of the railcar.
5. Cash expenditures in Months 2–5 are to cover the cost of the restoration of the railcar.
6. Month 6 is the first month the car will be in service. In this month, cash receipts are the prepayment of subscription fees, food concession fees, and ongoing revenue as reflected in the Profit and Loss Statement.

Exhibit A

1. How many months each year do you buy monthly commuter railroad tickets? (circle one)

    1   2   3   4   5   6   >6

2. What train station do you most frequently depart from in the morning?

    _____Philadelphia, 30th Street

    _____North Philadelphia

    _____Trenton

    _____Princeton

    _____Other _____

3. What train station do you travel *to* in the morning?

    _____Princeton

    _____Newark

    _____New York

    _____Other _____

4. Which Amtrak trains do you most frequently take in the morning?

Philadelphia   _____620A.M. _____650A.M. _____700A.M.

North   _____630A.M. _____700A.M. _____710A.M.
Philadelphia

Trenton   _____658A.M. _____741A.M.

Princeton   _____710A.M. _____753A.M.
Junction

5. Which trains do you most frequently take in the evening?

   1= Most frequent 2=Sometimes 3=Seldom 4=Never

(Answer all that apply)

New York   ____500P.M. ____506P.M.____518P.M.____530P.M.

Newark   ____512P.M. ____519P.M.____534P.M.____555P.M.

New York   ____605P.M. ____630P.M.____700P.M.____705P.M.

Newark   ____623P.M. ____643P.M.____712P.M.____720P.M.

6. If you could ride in a rail car to and from work that:

   a. Guaranteed you a seat;

   b. Offered breakfast in the morning and snacks/drinks in the
       evening;

   c. Offered cellular telephone service;

   d. Had a shoe shine service;

   Would you pay? (Circle all that apply)

   $350/month for this service   Y   N

   $400/month for this service   Y   N

   $450/month for this service   Y   N

   $500/month for this service   Y   N

A. If you could have breakfast on the railcar, what would you eat
    at least twice a week?

(Check all that apply)

_____Bagel   _____Coffee   _____Grapefruit juice

_____Muffin   _____Tea   _____Pancakes

_____Toast   _____Milk   _____Waffles

_____Eggs   _____Orange juice _____French toast

_____Sausage   _____Apple juice   _____Other_____

_____Bacon   _____Tomato juice _____

B. What would you drink at least twice a week in the evening?

_____

C. What snack/light dinner items would you eat in the evening?

_____

D. How often would you use a cellular telephone?

_____Not at all

_____Less than 1 hour/week

_____1–2 hours/week

_____2–3 hours/week

_____3–4 hours/week

_____4–5 hours/week

_____More

E. How often would you get your shoes shined?

1/week   _2/week_   _3/week_

$1.50/shine

$2.00/shine

F. Comments

_____

_____

_____

If you are interested in receiving more information about a service
   of this kind, please give us the following information:

Name_____

Street Address_____

City_____State_____Zip_____

Telephone_____

While this draft business plan was a very rough sketch of what needed to be done, Sam realized that many more things had to be investigated. His first priority was market research. Would the market truly ride on a luxury commuter railroad car to and from New York City? If they would, what price would they pay? How often would they ride it? What amenities would they truly want on board? And, which trains should it travel on in the morning and the evening?

In order to approach this market research intelligently, Sam consulted with a market research professor at the Wharton School, Kouzel Neitsbier, to help him design a proper survey instrument. The result of their collaboration is seen in Exhibit A on pages 78–80.

Sam got permission to implement the survey on board all of the commuter trains leaving Philadelphia. He left the surveys on the seats of the cars to make it look as if Amtrak was conducting the survey. The surveys yielded about an 88 percent response rate. Sam collected 80 names, addresses, and telephone numbers of people who would ride the train for an average of $400 per month.

Things looked quite optimistic, until Sam learned of an accident that occurred on an Amtrak train near Chase, Maryland. Remember, Sam had not yet purchased a railroad car. Yet, Amtrak felt that there may be a problem with the MaxRail line so it demanded that the insurance coverage of the railroad car be raised from $10 million to $25 million in liability coverage. The Johnson & Henry company, which insured most of the privately owned railroad cars in the United States, would not insure the MaxRail line for more than $10 million. In fact, Sam combed the world insurance markets and found no one willing to insure his yet-to-be-purchased railcar for $25 million—not even Lloyd's of London.

Sam decided that Amtrak's requirement of $25 million in insurance was discriminatory and something had to be done. He reasoned that he could apply pressure to the board of directors in order to change the policy. Sam enlisted the assistance of three members of the Amtrak board and decided to attend the public portion of the next board meeting to state his case. He and Benjamin Nevil took the train to Washington, D.C., and waited in the Amtrak board meeting room.

When the meeting commenced, Sam's most ardent supporter on the board, Charlie Smith, asked the chairman of Amtrak's board,

Bill Royal, to listen to what Sam had to say. Mr. Royal refused to hear him in the meeting, which started quite a to-do. Finally, Mr. Royal stated that he would talk to Sam after the meeting.

After the meeting, Mr. Royal told Sam that Amtrak would work something out in terms of the insurance coverage. That they did. As of the next day, Mr. Royal lowered Sam's insurance requirement to $10 million in coverage. Yet, at the same time, Amtrak reduced the length of the contract with MaxLine to one year.

All of a sudden, it didn't make sense to undertake the purchase and restoration of a railroad car. How could the financial partners recognize a payback on their investment in one year? But it did seem to be reasonable to consider renting a car. Sam began a search, in earnest, to see if there was any way that he could rent a car with the specifications needed for the "luxury" run. In fact, Sam did find a blunt-nosed observation car that he could rent for a year. It could carry only twenty people, though. As a consequence, looking at the profit and loss statement and the required revenues to break even, Sam found that he needed to charge $750 per person per month. Yet the survey he had run showed that riders would only pay an average of $400 per month for this service. What was he going to do?

Questions

1. What are the major and sub milestones involved in this venture from the start of the case?

2. What are the underlying assumptions in each of those major and sub milestones?

3. What is the order in which these major and sub milestones should be tested?

4. What are the resources needed to test each of the milestones you've outlined?

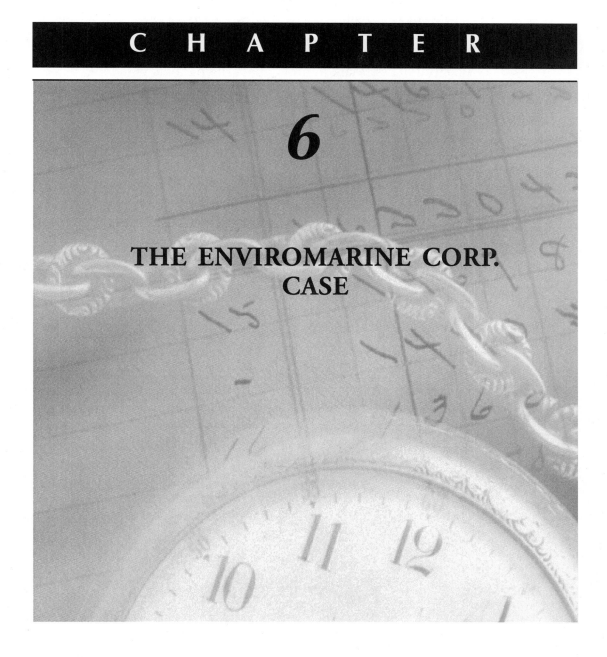

CHAPTER

6

THE ENVIROMARINE CORP. CASE

In January 1989, Stuart Butts and Rick Armstrong, the partners behind the Toronto-based Enviromarine Corp., were contemplating future plans for the company's proposed product, the VIRO Mark engine, a nonpolluting engine that ran on carbon dioxide. Engineering and marketing were in place, and the company had just received financing to complete the development, testing, patenting, and manufacture of 500 Mark III prototypes. The partners wondered where they should go from here.

THE VIRO ENGINE

The VIRO engine was powered by carbon dioxide (CO_2), a colorless, tasteless, odorless gas that is naturally present in the earth's atmosphere. CO_2 is also a waste product of industrial activities such as burning fossil fuels (e.g., gasoline, oil, and other petrochemical processes) and the manufacture of fertilizer. For "fuel," the VIRO engine uses canisters of liquid carbon dioxide. The carbon dioxide is liquified by compressing and cooling the gaseous CO_2 under high pressure.

Unlike the chemical energy released through combustion that powers a gasoline engine, the VIRO engine derives its power from mechanical energy. It works by converting liquid carbon dioxide back to gaseous carbon dioxide by gradually reducing the pressure and applying heat. The heat is provided to the outboard motor by the water. Any water temperature above freezing is adequate to heat the CO_2. The gas expands in the cylinder chamber and drives the piston. In contrast, in a conventional gasoline engine, the piston is driven by the explosion of the gasoline in the cylinder chamber.

Note: Case material of the Western School of Business Administration is prepared as a basis for classroom discussion and is not intended to present either an effective or ineffective handling of an administrative situation. This case was written by David McDiarmid under the supervision of Professor Russell M. Knight. Copyright (c) 1989, The University of Western Ontario.

ATTRACTIVE FEATURES OF THE VIRO ENGINE

The VIRO engine possessed a number of attractive features. Its principal advantage was that it was a nonpolluting motor. The motor required no combustion or chemical reaction. It released no noxious elements into the air or water, only CO_2.

The VIRO engine was also more ecologically sound than its gasoline counterpart in that it would reduce the amount of man-made CO_2 released into the atmosphere. Carbon dioxide emissions cause the warming of the atmosphere—the greenhouse effect. Each time a pound of gasoline is burnt, 3.14 pounds of carbon dioxide are produced. On the other hand, the VIRO uses the surplus CO_2 by-product of fertilizer manufacture and petrochemical processing industries as its source of energy. While a gasoline engine is contributing to the amount of man-made CO_2 in the atmosphere, the VIRO is using man-made CO_2 already produced. Therefore, for each pound of gasoline replaced by surplus CO_2, 3.14 pounds of CO_2 are prevented from being released into the atmosphere.

From an operating standpoint, the VIRO engine possessed several advantages. Since carbon dioxide is a noncombustible, nonexplosive gas, there was no risk of fire or explosion. The engine was principally constructed of aluminum, and consequently the production model, the Mark III, would weigh approximately 15 lbs. It had very few moving parts, no electric circuits and no sliding surfaces. Because the VIRO had no sliding parts, it required no lubrication. The engine started instantaneously: The mechanical energy was generated as soon as the valve on the CO_2 canister was opened. It generated essentially no sound when operating. It consumed only the amount of CO_2 released and consequently had an infinitely variable throttle (i.e., the amount of gas released corresponded exactly to the speed at which the motor ran).

Fertilizer manufacturing and petrochemical processing in Canada generate approximately 800,000 tons of CO_2 per year as a by-product. Three hundred thousand tons is presently used for such activities as welding, carbonation, refrigerating, and pressurizing, while the other 500,000 tons is released into the atmosphere. Therefore, a large surplus supply of CO_2 exists. To serve the existing market, the CO_2 is packaged in a number of conveniently sized canisters made of steel, aluminum, and more recently, plastic. Finally, CO_2 can be compressed into canisters using very inexpensive electric energy, making it an extremely inexpensive fuel: $12 a ton in Alberta. Consequently, the cost of operating a VIRO engine would be comparable to or better than the current cost of operating a gasoline-powered engine.

THE DEVELOPMENT OF THE VIRO AND ENVIROMARINE CORP.

The Initial Breakthrough

Rick Armstrong, the originator of the VIRO engine concept, had been a professional inventor since 1959. He had acted as an independent R&D firm, making "inventions to order." He had employed up to 20 engineers, designers, and technicians on his projects. Armstrong had been thinking about the idea of alternate energy sources for a number of years, including the possibility of carbon dioxide.

A number of engines that used CO_2 had previously been attempted, but all had fared poorly because they had used a standard piston engine. This type of engine could not keep the CO_2 warm enough since the gas would cool and condense as it pushed the piston down.

In 1985, Armstrong finally came up with a solution to the problem: a conical cylinder and piston instead of the traditional cylindrical ones. This proved to be the key breakthrough in developing the VIRO engine.

Armstrong assessed that a CO_2 engine would compare favorably with an equivalent gas-powered motor. He felt that a small, outboard fishing type motor would be the best application for the VIRO concept because of the high price of gas on lakes and the inefficiencies of existing outboard motors. He saw potential future applications of the VIRO engine in golf carts, houseboat motors, and personnel carriers for hazardous chemical plants. Wishing to find someone to help develop and market the engine, he built a plastic model of the motor.

The Partnership with Stuart Butts

In July of 1986, Armstrong was introduced to Stuart Butts by their patent agent. In addition to being a lawyer, Butts had undertaken a number of entrepreneurial ventures. A number of these had some sort of environmental concern aspect to them, such as a company that made underground storage tanks with a system to warn about leaks. Butts was interested in the motor and he and Armstrong agreed to work together on developing and marketing the product.

From July of 1986 to August of 1987, the partners worked on the project. Armstrong worked on refining the design of the engine, while Butts prepared a business plan and investigated possible financing sources. In October of 1986, Armstrong overcame a major problem in the conical piston/cylinder design. The problem was that the engine had a very short stroke time because of the shape of the piston/cylinder. Armstrong found a solution using a mechanical concept he developed called "nutation." Not only did this concept solve the VIRO short stroke problem, but Armstrong believed the concept would have a number of far-reaching effects in robotics and other areas.

On April 24, 1987, Butts convened a meeting with a cross-section of people in the business and science fields who had been exposed to the VIRO technology to get their opinions on the project. An outside engineering assessment was also obtained. This assessment would prove to be very useful in obtaining financing. On August 12, 1987, Enviromarine Corp. was incorporated. Butts was designated the president of the corporation.

INITIAL FINANCING

Butts had been seeking financing from a number of venture capitalists, with little success. None were willing to offer capital so early in the company's life. Many had reservations and doubts about the feasibility of the product. Finally, Butts was able to negotiate an underwriting agreement with Canarim Investment Corp. Ltd. on the 30th of August 1987. The financing would amount to $1.5 million, paid in two installments, and would give

Enviromarine Corp. sufficient funds to complete all phases of the VIRO engine development.

On September 15, 1987, the eight-member Board of Directors of Enviromarine Corp. agreed to invest $12,500 each in return for 40,000 common shares in the company, giving Enviromarine Corp. a total of $100,000. Butts was a member of the Board. On October 19, 1987, the Canarim Investment Corp. Ltd. informed Enviromarine that it was canceling the agreement to provide the $1.5 million. Butts immediately began to seek out other sources of financing. From December 1987 to June 1988, Enviromarine used the capital provided by the Board to assemble and test the first prototype of the outboard motor, the VIRO Mark I.

To enable the work on the first prototype to continue, seven of the eight members of the Board of Directors agreed to invest an additional $2,500 each on March 4, 1988, bringing their total stake in the VIRO to $15,000 apiece, or 50,000 common shares. Ten days later, on March 14, Butts closed a deal with the Ontario provincial government's Innovation Ontario Corporation. Innovation Ontario purchased a 20 percent stake in Enviromarine Corp. for $250,000. This association also lead to a working prototype of the VIRO engine being displayed in the Ontario Pavilion during the Economic Summit in Toronto in July, and, consequently, a lot of media exposure.

Armstrong and Butts believed that media support was a useful tool to lend credibility to the project, enhance corporate visibility, and reduce the level of disbelief that usually greets the unconventional idea of the VIRO engine. Media exposure could attract a number of interested parties ranging from potential investors to future customers. To facilitate communication between Enviromarine and the public, the company produced a number of promotional documents and business plans (Exhibit 1, page 92). An example of their "Good News" news letter appears in Exhibit 2 (page 93). A list of known media references to the company and the VIRO engine appears in Exhibit 3 (page 95).

In June of 1988, the first prototype, the VIRO Mark I, was completed and tested. The prototype fell far short of Armstrong's design specifications. The engine did not produce the hoped-for power output, and it operated in a jerky, noncontinuous fashion. Nevertheless, it demonstrated the feasibility of the concept and work was immediately started on a second version of the engine, the VIRO Mark II.

During the summer of 1988, Enviromarine made two important contacts. The first was with L. F. Burgess and Associates Ltd., a large Canadian marine manufacturer's representative. Burgress had over 30 years experience in the marine industry, and had offices in Halifax, Montreal, Toronto, and Vancouver. After talking to a number of outboard motor dealers, Burgess agreed to represent the VIRO in the Canadian market and manned a booth at the Dockside '88 marine show, explaining the VIRO engine.

The second contact was with Numet Engineering Ltd. of Peterborough, Ontario. The engineering firm agreed to work in conjuncture with Armstrong to complete the final stages of development of the second prototype, prepare engineering drawings for a commercial production model and assess the proposed production methods of the VIRO. Numet had over 17 years of engineering experience, and had worked for such clients as Atomic Energy of Canada, Canadian General Electric, and Ontario Hydro.

Unfortunately, the development of the second prototype, the VIRO Mark II, had to be suspended in May of 1988, due to a lack of funds.

FINAL FINANCING

At this point, Butts was talking to several large carbon dioxide producers about the possibility of providing financing. During this time, a copy of the VIRO newsletter and some press clippings fell into the hands of John Harries, the manager of the Gateway Enterprise Development Centre in Channel Port-aux-Basques, Newfoundland. The mandate of the Centre was to search out job opportunities for the citizens of Port-aux-Basques.

Harries contacted Enviromarine and was sent a copy of "The Breakthrough," a documentary video that described the VIRO engine. Harries in turn showed the video to a number of town officials of Port-aux-Basques. They agreed that the opportunity was an appropriate investment for some of the monies allocated to the town by virtue of the closing down of the Newfoundland railway at the end of September 1988. In return for the funding, the VIRO engine would be manufactured in the town.

On August 22, 1988, the president (Butts), one of the directors and the comptroller of Enviromarine met with the local officials in Port-aux-Basques. The comptroller intended to manage the production facility in Port-aux-Basques upon completion. The following week Harries and Butts traveled to St. Johns, Newfoundland, to meet with officials of the Atlantic Canada Opportunities Agency, the ultimate funding source. After this meeting, a working understanding of the agreement had been reached with all the apparent decision makers, but it took another four months to move the idea through the bureaucratic and political channels to obtain the actual funding.

This delay, besides causing frustration for the Enviromarine personnel, put in jeopardy aspects of the VIRO's patent position in other countries. Without patent funding, the protection for the new technology would have been lost. Harries was extremely instrumental in moving the proposal through the various levels of government as quickly as possible.

Finally, on December 30, 1988, Enviromarine received the first $100,000 of a total package of $1 million from the Community Diversification Corporation of the town of Port-aux-Basque.

THE FUTURE

With the marketing/distribution and engineering aspects already in place, Enviromarine now had the funds to complete the development, testing, patenting, and manufacture of 500 VIRO prototypes. The first 500 production models, the VIRO Mark III, were expected to be on the market for the summer of 1989. The motor would have a 9.9 h.p. engine, suitable for powering a fourteen foot aluminum boat. In January 1989, Armstrong and Butts were wondering where they should take Enviromarine and the VIRO engine from here.

Questions

1. What are the go/no go assumptions in Enviromarine?

2. What are the most critical milestones to prove the success of this venture? Order them in importance.

3. What are the high-impact assumptions that are and should be made and tested throughout this venture? Break them down by functional areas.

EXHIBIT 1   **ENVIROMARINE CORP. PRINCIPAL DOCUMENTS**

- Business plans that were simple and easy to understand. A number of business plans were produced at various stages in the process. The changes reflected changes in the stage of the project and, to a certain extent, answered the objections of the expected audience.

- VIRO "Good News" newsletters helped give a sense of direction to all of those in the know at various points in the progress of the development effort. By choosing the logo CO2 Good News, we headed off attacks on the technology on the basis that CO2 is "bad news."

- Documentary Video "The Breakthrough" produced May 25, 1988. "The Breakthrough" put the entire proposition of the VIRO succinctly, entertainingly, and in a timely manner. Timing can be everything. Taking an environmental bent before the summer of 1988 was a risky but important decision in the life of the project.

EXHIBIT 2   EXAMPLE OF THE ENVIROMARINE CORP. "GOOD NEWS" NEWSLETTER

VOL 1 NO 2   SEPTEMBER 88

THE VIRO AT DOCKSIDE

The carbon dioxide powered VIRO engine on display at DOCKSIDE is the original engineering prototype that was on display in the Ontario Pavilion during the Economic Summit in Toronto in July.

POLLUTION FREE

The VIRO requires no lubrication and its only emission is carbon dioxide, which makes it a non-polluting motor.

GASOLINE ADDS CO2

When gasoline is burnt one pound of gasoline combines with 14.8 pounds of air to produce 3.14 POUNDS OF CARBON DIOXIDE, 1.3 pounds of water, and 11.36 pounds of nitrogen, for a total weight of 15.8 pounds.

CO2 REDUCES CO2

For each pound of gasoline replaced by recycled carbon dioxide, used as a fuel, 3.14 pounds of carbon dioxide are actually prevented from being released into the atmosphere.

SILENT OPERATION

Because the VIRO works on the gradual release of rapidly expanding carbon dioxide there is no explosive process and essentially no noise of operation.

FIRST VIROS

The first production VIROS will be suitable for powering a fourteen foot aluminum boat. They are expected to be ideal for sport fishing boats or cottage run-abouts. The design target is a 9.9 h.p. motor.

ARTISTS CONCEPTION VIRO MARK 2

PRODUCTION ENGINEERING

Production engineering of the VIRO is being undertaken by Numet Engineering Ltd. of Peterborough. Their work will involve conducting a thorough analysis of the design, design specifications and the proposed production methods of the VIRO.

Numet brings over 17 years of engineering expertise to the VIRO team, having worked with such clients as Atomic Energy of Canada, Canadian General Electric and Ontario Hydro.

INDUSTRIAL DESIGN

The VIRO cover is being designed by the award-winning industrial design team of Vello Hubel and Peter Sepp. Their original design will take into account the ergonomic, functional and visual features of the VIRO.

PRODUCTION FOR 89

The initial production run of VIROS will be available for next summer.

MARKETING

L. F. Burgess and Associates Ltd., one of Canada's largest marine equipment representative organizations will be handling the sale and distribution of the VIRO in the Canadian marketplace. The Burgess organization brings over 30 years of experience in the marine trades industry and has offices in Halifax, Montreal, Toronto and Vancouver.

150 York Street Suite 900   Telephone (416) 363-0181
Toronto, Ontario   Telecopier (416) 363-3182
Canada. M5H 3S5

ENVIROMARINE CORP.

(continued)

EXHIBIT 2   EXAMPLE OF THE ENVIROMARINE CORP. "GOOD NEWS" NEWSLETTER

GOOD NEWS

TELL ME ABOUT CO2

Carbon dioxide, or CO2 if you prefer its chemical formulation, is a colourless, tasteless, odourless gas that is naturally present in the atmosphere and in the earth.

Commercial carbon dioxide is better than 99.9% pure.

In its early days as a commercial product, carbon dioxide was obtained from natural carbon dioxide gas wells and through the burning of fossil fuels. Today, most commercially distributed carbon dioxide is reclaimed as a waste product of ammonia and petrochemical production.

Liquid carbon dioxide is produced by compressing and cooling carbon dioxide gas under relatively high pressures. (800 lbs p.s.i.). Carbon dioxide is commercially available in high pressure canisters of various weights and sizes.

Because carbon dioxide is so widely used in such applications as welding, refrigerating, pressurizing and carbonating it is widely distributed in small quantities.

The cylinders used to store and transport carbon dioxide are subject to regular inspection to make sure they are safe from risks of cracking or leaking.

Because carbon dioxide is an inert gas there is no risk of fire or explosion.

A stylized CO2 constitutes Enviromarine's logo.

HOW DOES THE VIRO WORK?

The VIRO engine works by converting liquid carbon dioxide to gaseous carbon dioxide by reducing the pressure gradually while taking heat from the water. The heat is necessary to keep the carbon dioxide from recondensing as the pressure is released. Any water temperature above freezing provides an adequate supply of heat.

The VIRO propulsion process operates at optimum propellor blade speed to propulsive thrust. Only the carbon dioxide needed to drive a boat at a particular chosen speed is consumed. As a result, no fuel is consumed in "idle" and there is no inefficiency created by running the motor at a lower or greater speed.

HOW MUCH WORK CAN YOU GET OUT OF CARBON DIOXIDE?

A pound of CO2 vapour at saturated tank conditions contains 100 British Thermal Units (B.T.U.'s) of Useable Energy.

HOW DOES THAT COMPARE WITH GASOLINE?

It doesn't. The energy in gasoline is extracted through combustion. Chemical energy is released through the burning process. In the operation of the VIRO it is mechanical energy that is consumed. The carbon dioxide is stored under pressure at about 700 p.s.i. As the pressure is gradually released the carbon dioxide expands in volume by a factor over 100 as it progresses through the VIRO's cylinders and is exhausted. Nothing burns and there is no chemical reaction. The only release is the pure carbon dioxide.

(For the record, a pound of regular gasoline contains Approximately 20,000 BTU's of chemical energy. Only about 18% of this is useable.)

HOW DOES THE VIRO'S EFFICIENCY COMPARE WITH A GASOLINE ENGINE?

That depends on what you mean. Because the VIRO has such different operating characteristics from a gasoline engine it will fare better or worse depending upon how it is used. For example, the VIRO's efficiency will not change significantly with changes in speed. Because the VIRO works on a direct release of carbon dioxide it only consumes what it needs. It does not have an idle and no warm-up or start-up procedures are required.

The operator simply opens a valve releasing the desired amount of carbon dioxide and away she goes.

One measure of what to expect from the VIRO by way of performance can be described in the following example. Assume an aluminum boat 14 feet in length with two passengers. Assume a constant speed of 5 miles per hour. A 20 pound canister will last for three hours (15 miles). The VIRO probably can't beat the efficiency of a finely tuned gasoline engine operating at optimum speed, but these operating conditions are seldom attained.

WHAT ARE THE SIZE LIMITATIONS OF A VIRO?

There are none that we know of. Our next development project will probably be a VIRO of   about a 100 H.P.designed for use as a houseboat motor

EXHIBIT 3 LIST OF KNOWN ENVIROMARINE CORP. MEDIA REFERENCES

- David Crane, *The Toronto Star,* June 1, 1988
- Eric Reguly, *The Financial Post,* June 21, 1988
- Sandy Reilly, CBC World Service, News Feature Report, June 16, 1988 (Economic Summit)
- Mary Ferguson, CBC Morning Show, June 30, 1988
- Global Television News, July 1988 (Economic Summit)
- Anne Vanderhoff, *Cottage Life* magazine, Aug/Sept 1988
- Clue Trade Publication, September 1988
- *The Toronto Star,* September 13, 1988 (Dockside '88)
- John Borley, *Inside Canada,* October 2, 1988
- Pat Blandford, CFRB 1010 Radio, October 2, 1988
- Brian Nisbet, *Sailing Canada,* October 1988 edition
- Iain McMillan, *Canadian Yachting,* October 1988 edition
- Kim Zarzour, *The Toronto Star,* November 3, 1988
- Ian Cruickshank, *VISTA,* January 1989

CHAPTER

7

MILESTONE PLANNING FOR
SUCCESSFUL VENTURES
QuickStart

OUTLINE

Milestone Planning for
Successful Ventures
Before You Start
Requirements
Installing Milestone
Planning for Successful
Ventures
Milestones
Using Milestone Planning
for Successful Ventures
    Major Milestones
    Sub Milestones
    Creating Milestones
    Opening an Existing
    Milestone Document
    Adding Major and Sub
    Milestones
    Selecting Major and Sub
    Milestones
    Changing a Milestone
    Template

Saving a Milestone
Template
Assumptions
Show Findings
Editing Findings
Exiting Findings
Primary Responsibility
Quantitative Information
Involvements
Adding Names
Using the Involvement
Palette
Applying the
Involvement Pair
Reporting
    Creating a Report
    Using Settings
    Editing the Report
    Exiting the Editor
    Generating Charts

MILESTONE PLANNING FOR SUCCESSFUL VENTURES

You are about to experience a breakthrough in management technique. Milestone Planning for Successful Ventures' simplified approach allows you to successfully control new ventures, develop new products and services, and control long-term projects. It permits you to quickly and easily assign responsibilities, set assumptions and costs, keep notes, and monitor progress. And, the program presents all information on one screen in an easy-to-read format that allows you to quickly review and update a project.

This is more than a software program, though. It relies on a new concept, a paradigm that consists of milestone planning techniques to successfully manage ventures and projects. It offers more than traditional project management programs that apply critical path management (CPM) techniques to ventures and projects. These rely on a specific order of events that must happen in a predetermined sequence before a project can reach completion. Milestone Planning for Successful Ventures provides the method you need to control the more typical, non-CPM projects and ventures. It will force you to re-evaluate your traditional thought processes, but the reward for doing so is rich.

Based on a paper written by two college professors, Ian MacMillan and Zenas Block, published in the *Harvard Business Review,* Milestone Planning for Successful Ventures enables you to assemble all the information gained during a process. It manages ventures and projects based on experience. Far too many times the bulk of the information gained while a venture or project develops isn't captured. We get too busy to document the process properly, or we decide that we will document the project only on a weekly basis, losing track of all the small decisions that allowed the project to move forward. Instead, this information goes into the personal knowledge base of the manager involved.

Milestone Planning for Successful Ventures helps you impose discipline on your ventures and projects and helps capture all the data. More important, Milestone Planning for Successful Ventures simplifies your job, automates reporting, and saves time.

BEFORE YOU START

Milestone Planning for Successful Ventures uses Microsoft Windows, and this manual assumes some basic computer experience. If you are unfamiliar with using a mouse, Microsoft Windows, or pull-down menus, check the Microsoft Windows manual for further instructions.

REQUIREMENTS

Milestone Planning for Successful Ventures requires the following:

- A DOS-based system using 80286 or more powerful processor
- At least 2M bytes of memory

- A hard disk drive
- Microsoft Windows, version 3.0 or later

You also need the Milestone Planning for Successful Ventures diskette and a formatted 5.25-inch or 3.5-inch, high-density diskette.

INSTALLING MILESTONE PLANNING FOR SUCCESSFUL VENTURES

Always make a working copy of the master diskette and use that copy to install the program. For information on how to copy diskettes, refer to your DOS manual.

To install Milestone Planning for Successful Ventures on a hard disk:

 Using the Mouse

1. Place the first Milestone Planning for Successful Ventures diskette into the diskette drive.
2. From the DOS prompt (C:), enter **SHARE** (ENTER) .
3. Start Windows by typing **WIN** (ENTER) .
4. Activate the Windows Program Manager by clicking the PRO-GRAM MANAGER icon twice.
5. Select the File pull-down menu on the Program Manager by clicking on FILE in the command bar.
6. Select RUN from the File pull-down menu .
7. Type A:\INSTALL. **Note:** This assumes the diskette is in drive A:; if the diskette is in drive B:, type B:\INSTALL.
8. Click the OK button.
9. Follow the instructions on the screen and answer prompts until the installation is complete.
10. Start Milestones by double-clicking on the Milestones icon.

 Using the Keyboard

1. Place the Milestone Planning for Successful Ventures diskette into the diskette drive.

2. From the DOS prompt (C:), enter **SHARE** (ENTER).

3. Start Windows by typing **WIN** (ENTER).

4. Activate the Windows Program Manager by pressing (SHIFT) (ESC).

5. Maximize the Program Manager by entering (X).

6. Select the File menu on the Program Manager by entering (ALT) (F).

7. Select RUN from the File menu by keying (R).

8. Type A:\INSTALL. **Note:** This assumes the diskette is in drive A:; if the diskette is in drive B:, type B:\INSTALL.

9. Tab to the OK button and press enter— (TAB) (ENTER).

10. Follow the instructions and answer prompts on the screen until the installation is complete.

11. Start Milestones by tabbing to the Milestones icon and pressing enter— (TAB) (ENTER).

Note: Once you install Milestone Planning for Successful Ventures, printer options, network options, and backup functions can be run from the command bar. The options are found on the Edit sub menu under the Preferences command.

MILESTONES

MacMillan and Block state that major events or milestones exist in all ventures and projects and that there are no more than 10 major milestones. They also believe that the same major milestones repeat in a wide variety of ventures and projects. Thus, all ventures encounter the same 10 milestones:

1. Concept/Product Test

2. Complete Prototype

3. First Financing

4. Pilot Product/Plant Operations

5. Initial Market Test

6. Production Startup

7. Bellwether Sale

8. First Significant Price Change

9. First Redesign or Redirection

10. First Competitive Action

While the first six milestones generally occur in the order listed, the remaining four milestones can occur at any time and in any order. This differs from traditional CPM planning techniques where managers frequently end up handling multiple developments simultaneously, which can prevent the proper documentation of decisions and events.

Also important to Milestone Planning for Successful Ventures is the concept that each major milestone has multiple sub milestones. These are the individual processes that you must perform to accomplish the major milestone. You can define an unlimited number of sub milestones.

Each milestone corresponds to a series of assumptions. These assumptions, best phrased as questions, outline all the elements that need to happen for the project or venture to progress. For example, under the Concept/Product Test milestone you must determine if the concept or product you want to launch has merit. The questions for this milestone would include: Are the attributes defined properly? Is the market defined properly? Is it operationally feasible to consider the production of this concept or product with these attributes?

Similarly, the complete prototype milestone requires answers for such questions as: Does the product need refinement? Does it satisfy market needs? Can the product be built and offered at a price the market will accept?

This forces you to make explicit assumptions before you proceed to define the next milestone. Most projects and ventures start with assumptions, but these basic assumptions are rarely expressed in concrete terms and tied to measurable goals. For example, product developers may state that they believe a market exists, but by forcing explicit assumptions, those product developers need to define market needs by segments, size of market, and methods of selling in that market. At the same time, it encourages you to group all the explicit assumptions for each major or sub milestone.

USING MILESTONE PLANNING FOR SUCCESSFUL VENTURES

When you first start Milestone Planning for Successful Ventures, the Milestone Planner screen appears.

```
┌─────────────────────────────────────────────────────────────────┐
│ ─              Milestone Planner - [Basic]                    ▼  │
│  File   Edit   Planner   Create                           Help   │
│  Major Milestones      Primary Responsibility                    │
│  ┌─────────────────┬─┐ ┌──────────────────────────────────┐      │
│  │A. Concept/Product Test│±│ │Bernard David                 │      │
│  └─────────────────┴─┘ └──────────────────────────────────┘      │
│  Sub Milestones        Attributes                                │
│  ┌─────────────────┬─┐                      Plan        Actual   │
│  │Sub Milestone 1   │±│         Cost:│$ 15000.00│  │$ 13576.00│  │
│  └─────────────────┴─┘                                           │
│  Assumptions            Days to Completion:│85      │ │105     │ │
│  ┌─────────────────┬─┐     Start Date:│1/1/1994│   │1/1/1994│   │
│  │This is the assumption│▲│  End Date:│3/1/1994│   │4/1/1994│   │
│  │box where you list  │ │                                        │
│  │explicit assumptions│ │  Involvements                          │
│  │                    │ │  Name              Involvement Level   │
│  │                    │▼│  Bernard David         Approval        │
│  └─────────────────┴─┘ Gerald Williams        Information        │
│  ┌───────────────────┐  Outside Service Bureau Support           │
│  │   Show Findings    │                                          │
│  └───────────────────┘                                          │
│  (c) Educational Software, Inc. 1990-1993  │⇤│ │⇐│ │⇒│ │⇥│      │
└─────────────────────────────────────────────────────────────────┘
```

This screen serves as a data entry vehicle and allows you to review each major and related sub milestone quickly and easily. This unique view also permits you to interactively record the project's progress and record comments without leaving the Milestone Planner screen.

Most functions use the command bar at the top, which follows the Windows approach of listing active commands in regular typeface and inactive commands in gray typeface in the pull-down menus.

Using the command bar

A command bar runs across the top of the Milestone Planner screen.

You call pull-down menus under each command by pointing to the command with the mouse and clicking. You also can call the pull-down menus using the following key combinations:

File Menu	⟨ALT⟩	⟨F⟩
Edit Menu	⟨ALT⟩	⟨E⟩
Planner Menu	⟨ALT⟩	⟨P⟩
Create Menu	⟨ALT⟩	⟨T⟩

You can then select the proper item on the pull-down menus with a mouse or with keystrokes.

MAJOR MILESTONES

The upper left-hand section of the Milestone Planner screen identifies the active Major Milestone.

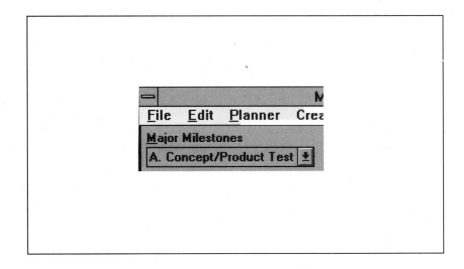

All other information in other areas of the screen relate to that Milestone, and information changes when you activate another Milestone. You highlight this area by clicking on the box with a mouse or you can move around the screen by pressing (TAB).

Clicking the mouse on the small pull-down indicator at the right of the Major Milestones box displays the Major Milestones in alphabetical order in a pull-down box.

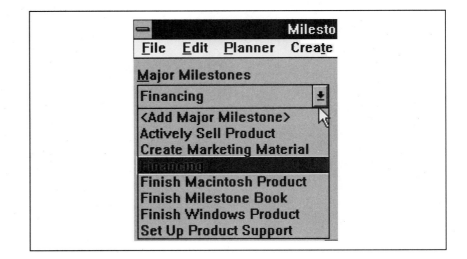

You can then select a milestone by pointing and clicking on it or using the cursor keys on the keyboard. There is no key alternative for calling the list of Major Milestones, although you can review the list one at a time by using the up and down cursor keys.

SUB MILESTONES

The tasks that make up Sub Milestones are listed in a box below the Major Milestones box. Clicking the mouse on the box or tabbing to the box with the keyboard highlights the box, and all Sub Milestones related to the active Major Milestones display in alphabetical order when you click the pull-down indicator on the right-hand side of the box.

After the pull-down box appears, you can display a specific Sub Milestone by pointing and clicking on that Sub Milestone with the mouse or using the keyboard cursor keys.

CREATING MILESTONES

The Milestone Document starts with a Milestone Set—a list of events that must be accomplished to reach specific goals. The Milestone Set is key to successful projects and ventures.

Using the Mouse

The following steps show how to create a new Milestone Set.

1. Select CREATE in the command bar. This calls a pull-down menu.

<u>F</u>ile	<u>E</u>dit	<u>P</u>lanner	Cre<u>a</u>te		
			<u>M</u>ilestone Templates...	Ctrl+M	
			<u>A</u>ssumptions...	Ctrl+A	
			<u>I</u>nvolvements...	Ctrl+I	
			<u>R</u>eports...	Ctrl+R	

---

2. Click on MILESTONE TEMPLATE in the pull-down menu.

Milestone Template Editor

<u>F</u>ile   <u>E</u>dit   <u>H</u>elp

Current <u>T</u>emplate Name

Davids's Milestones   <u>C</u>ancel   <u>O</u>K

Major Milestone 1	Major Milestone 6
Major Milestone 2	Major Milestone 7
Major Milestone 3	Major Milestone 8
Major Milestone 4	Major Milestone 9
Major Milestone 5	Major Milestone 10

The resulting screen, called the Milestone Template Editor, displays 10 blanks for milestones. After you have established some Milestone Sets, the blanks will be filled with the Milestones associated with the active document. To start a new Milestone Document in the Milestone Template Editor:

3. Click on FILE in the command bar on the Milestone Template Editor.

File Edit	
New Template	**Ctrl+N**
Open Template	**Ctrl+O**
Save	**Ctrl+S**
Save As...	
Rename Template	
Delete Template	
Exit Editor	**Ctrl+X**

4. Select NEW from the pull-down menu.

5. The system prompts you to name the new Milestone Set, and it accepts any name up to 40 characters in length (including spaces).

Add New Milestone Template

New Template Name

[Cancel] [OK]

Use meaningful names for the Milestone Set. Milestone Planning for Successful Ventures uses templates to quickly build new Milestone Sets. After you create a Milestone Set, you can reuse it as a basis for planning new projects and ventures. Therefore, you will want to recognize it from a list of names without opening the Milestone Set and looking at the contents.

Note: The system will not allow you to reuse any names already in use for another Milestone Set. If a duplicate name is used, a warning block appears. To clear the warning box, click the OK button.

Hint: All Major and Sub Milestones are listed in alphabetical order. You many want your milestones to appear in a specific order. We recommend that you precede all Major and Sub Milestones with "A." for the first milestone, "B. " for the second one, and so on. This will give the sort order you want and allow you to change that order easily later by editing the name of the milestone.

6. When Milestone Planning for Successful Ventures accepts the new name, it appears in the Name box and the milestone boxes are blank. You can enter up to 10 milestones by clicking on a blank box and entering a name that is up to 33 characters. When you are finished,

7. Click on the OK button. If you want to cancel your efforts to this point, click on the CANCEL button. When you click on the OK button, the system prompts you to verify that you want the changes saved.

8. Click the OK button to save the new Milestone Set. Click the NO button to continue with the session without saving the new Milestone Set; the CANCEL button returns to the Milestone Planner screen with no changes.

Milestone Planning for Successful Ventures now returns to the original Milestone Planner screen. However, the new Milestone Set will not appear on this screen until it is opened. See Opening an Existing Milestone Document following the Using the Keyboard section.

Using the Keyboard

To define a new Milestone Set:

1. Select CREATE from the command bar by entering (ALT) (T).
2. Select the Milestone Template from the pull-down menu by entering (CTRL) (M).

The resulting screen, called the Milestone Template Editor, displays 10 blank boxes for Milestones. These blanks are filled with the current Milestones.

To start a new Milestone Document in the Milestone Template Editor screen:

1. Enter (ALT) (F).
2. Enter (N).

   Alternately, you can go directly to the Add New Milestone Template by entering (CTRL) (N). The system prompts you to name the new Milestone Set.

3. Enter any name up to 40 characters long (including spaces). Don't worry about length. Most entries will fall far below 40 characters. Also, you should use a meaningful name for the Milestone Set. Milestone Planning for Successful Ventures uses templates to allow you to quickly build new Milestone Sets. After you create a Milestone Set, you can reuse it as a basis for planning new projects and ventures. Therefore, you will want to recognize it from a list of names without opening the Milestone Set and looking at the contents.

   The system will not allow you to reuse any names already in use for another Milestone Set. If a duplicate name is used, a warning block appears. Acknowledge the error and continue by hitting (ENTER).

4. If Milestone Planning for Successful Ventures accepts the new name, it appears in the Name box and the milestone boxes are blank. You can enter up to 10 milestones by tabbing to a blank box and entering a name that is up to 33 characters long.

To move the cursor forward through the boxes and the Cancel and OK buttons, press (TAB). (SHIFT) (TAB) moves the cursor backward.

5. When you are finished, press (ENTER). Optionally, you can tab until the OK button is highlighted and press (ENTER). If you want to cancel this effort, tab until the CANCEL button is highlighted and press (ENTER). If you pressed OK, the system will prompt you to verify that you want the changes saved.

6. If you want to make the changes, press (ENTER). If you want to continue without saving the new Milestone Set, tab to highlight the No button and press (TAB) (ENTER). To return to the Milestone Template Editor, tab twice to highlight the CANCEL button and press enter— (TAB) (TAB) (ENTER). Milestone Planning for Successful Ventures returns to the original Milestone Planner screen. Your new Milestone Set will not appear on this screen until it is opened.

OPENING AN EXISTING MILESTONE DOCUMENT

To review a project, the Milestone Set must be opened from the Milestone Planner screen. This is a simple process, aided by pull-down menus and quick access methods.

Using the Mouse

1. Click on FILE in the command bar. A pull-down menu appears.

File	Edit	Planner	Create
New			Ctrl+N
Open...			Ctrl+O
Save			Ctrl+S
Save As...			
Page Setup...			
Printer Setup...			
Delete Milestone Set...			
Rename Milestone Set...			
Exit Milestone Program			Ctrl+X

If this is the first time you are using a Milestone Set:

2. Select NEW from the pull-down menu and click the mouse.

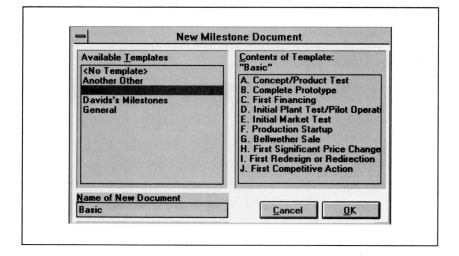

The New Milestone Document screen appears. In the left-hand box, the screen lists all available templates in alphabetical order while the right-hand box shows the Milestone Set associated with the highlighted template. You can browse the templates by using the cursor bar next to the box or by clicking on a specific template. Also, you can move the highlight by keying the first letter of a template's name.

3. To activate the new Milestone Template, enter a unique name in the Name of New Document box. **Hint:** This is an easy way to reuse Milestone Sets already created for another project. To ensure that you can easily access this Milestone Set in the future, save the Milestone Planning Document:

4. Click on FILE in the command bar.

File	Edit	Planner	Create
New			Ctrl+N
Open...			Ctrl+O
Save			Ctrl+S
Save As...			
Page Setup...			
Printer Setup...			
Delete Milestone Set...			
Rename Milestone Set...			
Exit Milestone Program			Ctrl+X

5. Select SAVE from the pull-down menu.

If you have already used a Milestone Set or followed the previous instructions:

1. Select FILE in the command bar to call the pull-down menu.

File	Edit	Planner	Create
New			Ctrl+N
Open...			Ctrl+O
Save			Ctrl+S
Save As...			
Page Setup...			
Printer Setup...			
Delete Milestone Set...			
Rename Milestone Set...			
Exit Milestone Program			Ctrl+X

2. Click on OPEN in the pull-down menu. The Open Milestone Document screen appears with all Milestone Planning Documents listed in alphabetical order.

Open Milestone Document

Documents

- **A Basic Project**
- **A Second Milestone Set**
- **A Third Milestone Set**
- **Basic**
- **General Milestones**
- **Master Milestones**
- **Milestones/Mac&Zenas**
- **The Other Project**
- **Venture Milestones**

[Cancel]

[OK]

---

3. Highlight the document you want by clicking on it. You can also use cursor keys to navigate the list or enter the first letter of the Milestone Document you want to open.

4. Click the OK button. If you want to return to the Milestone Planner screen without opening a new Milestone Set, click on CANCEL.

Using the Keyboard

1. Select the FILE pull-down menu in the command bar by entering Ⓕ. If this is the first time you are using a Milestone Set:

2. Select NEW from the pull-down menu by keying Ⓝ.

   The New Milestone Document screen appears. In the left-hand box, the screen lists all available templates in alphabetical order while the right-hand box shows the Milestone Set associated with the highlighted template. You can browse the templates by using the cursor bar next to the box or by clicking on a specific template. Also, you can move the highlight by keying the first letter of a template's name.

   Hint: This is an easy way to reuse Milestone Sets already created for another project.

3. To activate the new Milestone Template, enter a unique name in the Name of New Document box. To ensure that you can easily access this Milestone Set in the future, save the Milestone Planning Document:

4. Key (ALT) (F).

5. Select SAVE by hitting (S).

If you have already used a Milestone Set or followed the previous instructions:

1. Call the pull-down menu under FILE in the command bar with (ALT) (F).

2. Key (O) to select OPEN in the pull-down menu. The Open Milestone Document screen appears with all Milestone Planning Documents listed in alphabetical order.

3. Highlight the document by cursoring to it.

4. (TAB) until the OK button is highlighted. Hit (ENTER).

If you want to return to the Milestone Planner screen without opening a new Milestone Set, (TAB) until the CANCEL button is highlighted and hit (ENTER).

ADDING MAJOR AND SUB MILESTONES

You can add Major and Sub Milestones on the main Milestone Planner screen or through utilities. This allows you to set milestones quickly, and add sub milestones as the project or venture progresses.

Using the Mouse

1. Click on the arrow at the right of the Major Milestones box or the Sub Milestones box, depending on which milestone you need to add.

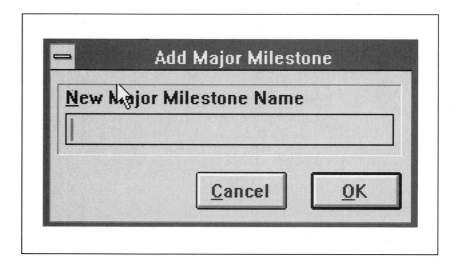

A listing of all Major Milestones or Sub Milestones appears in a pull-down menu along with the entry <ADD MAJOR MILE-STONE> or <ADD SUB MILESTONE>.

2. Click on the <ADD MAJOR MILESTONE> or <ADD SUB MILE-STONE> entry. This generates the Add Major Milestone or Add Sub Milestone screen.

3. Type the name of the new milestone. It can be up to 33 characters (including spaces) long.

4. Click OK to add the milestone. Click the CANCEL button to return to the original screen without adding the milestone.

Reminder: The current version of Milestone Planning for Successful Ventures does not support more than 10 Major Milestones. Attempts to do so will cause the program to run erratically. There is no limit on Sub Milestones.

You can also use PLANNER and CREATE in the command bar to add new milestones.

Using the Keyboard

1. Cursor through the Major Milestones box or the Sub Milestones selections using the arrow keys, depending on which milestone you need to add.

2. The Add Major Milestone or Add Sub Milestone screen will automatically appear when you cursor to the <ADD MAJOR MILESTONE> or <ADD SUB MILESTONE> selection.

3. Type the name of the new milestone. It can be up to 33 characters (including spaces) long.

4. ⌷TAB⌶ to highlight the OK button and hit ⌷ENTER⌶ to add the milestone. ⌷TAB⌶ to highlight the CANCEL button and hit ⌷ENTER⌶ to return to the original screen without adding the milestone.

You can also use PLANNER and CREATE in the command bar to add new milestones.

SELECTING MAJOR AND SUB MILESTONES

To view milestones and associated data or to change or delete milestones, you need to select the specified data. The active Major Milestone and Sub Milestone appear in the milestone boxes in the Milestone Planner screen. There are two ways to select a different milestone.

Using the Mouse

1. Click on the arrow at the right of the Major Milestones box or the Sub Milestones box, depending on which milestone you need to add.

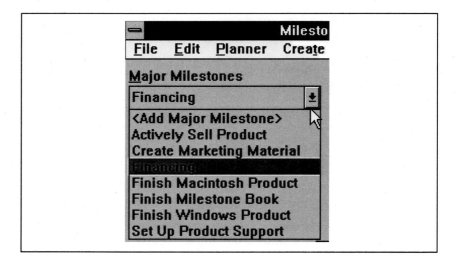

2. An alphabetical listing of all Major Milestones or Sub Milestones appears in a pull-down box.

3. Click on the Major Milestone or Sub Milestone you want to change. You also can navigate this list by typing the first letter of a milestone.

You can also select a Major Milestone or Sub Milestone from the Milestone Palette.

Using the Keyboard

You can view Major Milestones or Sub Milestones by using the arrow keys to cursor through the list. As an alternative, it may be easier to use the Milestone Palette.

1. Call the PLANNER pull-down menu in the command bar by entering ⟨ALT⟩ ⟨P⟩.

2. Select MILESTONE PALETTE from the pull-down menu by keying ⟨M⟩. This generates the Milestone Palette screen, which lists all Major Milestones and Sub Milestones in alphabetical order.

3. Highlight the milestone you want to load. You can navigate through the list by typing the first letter of a Major Milestone or using the cursor keys.

4. ⬭TAB⬭ to highlight the SELECT button and hit ⬭ENTER⬭. If you want to return to the screen without making a selection, ⬭TAB⬭ to highlight the CANCEL button and hit ⬭ENTER⬭.

You can also select a Major Milestone or Sub Milestone from the Milestone Palette.

CHANGING A MILESTONE TEMPLATE

The Milestone Template Editor allows you to edit Milestone Templates. Each entry can be edited by moving the cursor to that entry. If you are using a mouse, you can highlight a box by clicking on it. The Tab key also moves the cursor from box to box.

Once inside the box, you can move the cursor within a word by clicking at the desired position. Two clicks highlight the entire word, and holding the left mouse button down while dragging the cursor across a group of characters will highlight those characters.

In addition to implementing the basic mouse functions, the Milestone Template Editor also includes basic editing functions. These are accessed through the Command Menu.

Using the Mouse

Click on EDIT in the Milestone Template Editor command bar. A pull-down menu appears.

<u>F</u>ile	<u>E</u>dit	
	<u>U</u>ndo	Alt+Bksp
	Cu<u>t</u>	Shift+Del
	<u>C</u>opy	Ctrl+Ins
	<u>P</u>aste	Shift+Ins
	Clea<u>r</u>	Ctrl+Del
	Select <u>A</u>ll	

The following functions can be accessed by clicking on the associated commands in the pull-down menu.

Undo	Changes the document to the way it appeared prior to the last command or keystroke. This command affects only the most recent action.
Cut	Deletes any highlighted text and places the deleted text into a buffer for later use. The buffer holds only the latest CUT or COPY text block.
Copy	Copies any highlighted text and places that text block into a buffer for later use. Like the CUT operation, the buffer holds only that latest text block that is cut or copied.
Paste	Places any text in the buffer into the document at the position of the cursor.
Clear	Erases all highlighted text. The deleted text is not copied into the buffer.
Select All	Highlights the entire box where the cursor resides.

 Using the Keyboard

Call the EDIT pull-down menu in the Milestone Template Editor command bar by entering (ALT) (E).

The following functions can be accessed by clicking on the associated commands in the pull-down menu.

Undo (ALT) (E) (U)	Changes the document to the way it appeared prior to the last command or keystroke. This command affects only the most recent action.
Cut (ALT) (E) (T)	Deletes any highlighted text and places the deleted text into a buffer for later use. The buffer holds only the latest CUT or COPY text block.
Copy (ALT) (E) (C)	Copies any highlighted text and places that text block into a buffer for later use. Like the CUT operation, the buffer holds only that latest text block that is cut or copied.
Paste (ALT) (E) (P)	Places any text in the buffer into the document at the position of the cursor.

Clear
ⒶⓁⓉ Ⓔ Ⓡ   Erases all highlighted text. The deleted text is not
                   copied into the buffer.

Select All
ⒶⓁⓉ Ⓔ Ⓢ   Highlights the entire box where the cursor resides.

SAVING A MILESTONE TEMPLATE

You can either save the active Milestone Template under its current name or save it under another name that you assign.

Using the Mouse

Click on FILE in the Milestone Template Editor command bar. This
generates a pull-down menu.

File Edit	
New Template	Ctrl+N
Open Template	Ctrl+O
Save	Ctrl+S
Save As...	
Rename Template	
Delete Template	
Exit Editor	Ctrl+X

If you want to use the same name, select SAVE from the pull-down
menu. This action replaces the old data with the new data. If you want
to use a different name, (1) select SAVE AS from the pull-down menu.
This option creates a separate Milestone Template with a new name.
The system presents the Save As screen that asks you to name the new
file; (2) Enter the name for the revised Milestone Template.

SAVE AS

Save Milestone Template As:

Davids's Milestones

Cancel   **O**K

To save the file, click on OK to save the new file. If you want to return to the Milestone Template Editor without saving the file, click the CANCEL button.

Using the Keyboard

Call the FILE pull-down menu in the Milestone Template Editor command bar by entering ⒜ALT⒝ ⒡F⒝. If you want to use the same name, select SAVE from the pull-down menu by keying ⒮S⒝. This action replaces the old data with the new data. If you want to use a different name, (1) Select SAVE AS from the pull-down menu by hitting ⒜A⒝. This option creates a separate Milestone Template with a new name. The system presents the Save As screen that asks you to name the new file; (2) Enter the name for the revised Milestone Template.

To save the file, highlight the OK button and hit ⒠ENTER⒡ to save the new file. If you want to return to the Milestone Template Editor without saving the file, highlight the CANCEL button and hit ⒠ENTER⒡.

ASSUMPTIONS

The text area toward the bottom of the left-hand column of the Milestone Planner screen lets you record the assumptions that support each milestone. Assumptions include the explicit goals that must be met in each Major Milestone for the project or venture to proceed successfully. These are the explicit assumptions, discussed earlier, that need constant evaluation. Obviously, you must monitor and revise your assumptions as the project or venture progresses.

You can highlight the Assumptions box by clicking on it with the mouse or tabbing to it with the keyboard.

When the box is active, a character cursor appears inside the box. All data entered in the Assumptions box keys to a specific Major Milestone or Sub Milestone. This allows the system to display only related information, making it easier for you to look at a project and quickly review its progress.

The Assumptions box in the lower left-hand quadrant of the Milestone Planner Screen can operate as a simple text field. Clicking on the box with the mouse or tabbing to the box using the keyboard generates a cursor. You can enter text at this point, and the text will automatically wrap around as you enter it.

Once text exists in the box, the EDIT function in the command box is activated. It works the same as the editing function under the Milestone Template Editor.

Each assumption remains tied to the specific Sub Milestone it was entered under. This means that each time you call that Sub Milestone, the assumption will appear. The assumption can be edited or added to any time it is visible in the Assumptions box by clicking on the box or tabbing to the box.

As you become more familiar with Milestone Planning for Successful Ventures, you will want to use the Assumptions Palette.

SHOW FINDINGS

As you review a project, it is necessary to keep detailed notes that extend beyond the capacity of the assumptions. The Show Findings button at the bottom of the left-hand column in the Milestone Planner screen calls a separate text screen for notes.

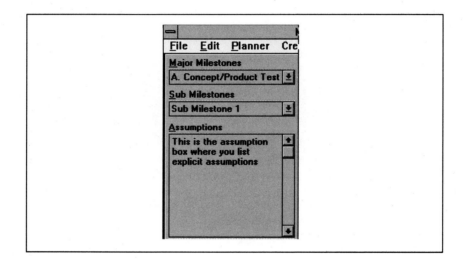

Additionally, the text screen features a button that invokes a word processor. The default word processor is Microsoft Write, but you can invoke other word processors by changing the preference setting. You can also access the Show Findings feature through the PLANNER pull-down menu.

EDITING FINDINGS

If any text exists, it displays in the Edit Findings box (called through the Show Findings button). You can edit the text in this box or enter new text in the box. If you want to access the full power of a word processor (Microsoft Write is the default processor), click on the WORD PROCESSOR button. You also can type your comments and copy the selected text to the clipboard and paste it in the Show Findings box.

EXITING FINDINGS

If you have entered new text or edited existing text in the Edit Findings box, click the OK button and the system saves the text. The CANCEL button returns you to the Milestone Planner screen without saving any changes you have made.

From the keyboard, you need to highlight the OK button using the tab key. Once the OK button is highlighted, hit the ENTER key to save the changes and return to the Milestone Planner screen. You also can tab to the CANCEL button and hit enter to return to the Milestone Planner screen without saving changes.

PRIMARY RESPONSIBILITY

If an individual has primary responsibility for completion of a major or sub milestone, that individual bears the greatest responsibility for completing them.

The box toward the upper right-hand corner of the Milestone Planner screen displays the name of the person who has responsibility for the Major Milestone or Sub Milestone task.

```
┌────────────────────────────────────────────────────────────┐
│                                                            │
│                                                            │
│  ┌──────────────────────────────────────────────────────┐ │
│  │ ⊟ │        Milestone Planner - [Basic]          │ ▼ │ │
│  │ File   Edit   Planner   Create              Help   │ │
│  │ Major Milestones        Primary Responsibility      │ │
│  │ A. Concept/Product Test ±  Bernard David            │ │
│  │                                                      │ │
│  │                                                      │ │
│  │                                                      │ │
│  └──────────────────────────────────────────────────────┘ │
│                                                            │
└────────────────────────────────────────────────────────────┘
```

You can edit the name on screen or change it using a user-defined palette with names. You highlight this box by clicking it with the mouse or tabbing to it on the keyboard. Milestone Planning for Successful Ventures also permits you to assign the level of involvement for other primary participants, as discussed in the Involvement section.

QUANTITATIVE INFORMATION

The boxes in the middle of the right-hand column provide space to record the projected cost, project duration, and scheduled start and end dates. Fields showing the actual costs, duration, and start and end dates are positioned next to the projected fields.

You simply tab to the field you want to complete or click on that field once with the mouse pointer. The fields automatically format your input to conform to dollars or dates. This provides the quickest and easiest ways to set a schedule and costs. More important, it offers instant comparisons between the project's planned budget and schedule and the actual cost and progress as the project or venture continues.

INVOLVEMENTS

People can play important roles in a project or venture without having primary responsibility. The Involvements box at the bottom of the right-hand column displays the names of everyone who contributes to the milestone and shows their level of involvement.

This ensures that everyone working on a project understands their roles. Like the other boxes, you can highlight this box by clicking on it with the mouse or tabbing to the area using the keyboard.

ADDING NAMES

You need to build a master list of names that identifies everyone who may have involvements in your project or venture. Also, as the project or venture progresses, you will need to expand this list of names.

Using the Mouse

1. Click on CREATE in the Milestone Planner screen command bar. This generates a pull-down menu.

<u>F</u>ile	<u>E</u>dit	<u>P</u>lanner	Crea<u>t</u>e		
			<u>M</u>ilestone Templates...		Ctrl+M
			<u>A</u>ssumptions...		Ctrl+A
			<u>I</u>nvolvements...		Ctrl+I
			<u>R</u>eports...		Ctrl+R

2. Select INVOLVEMENTS from the pull-down menu. This creates the Modify Names screen.

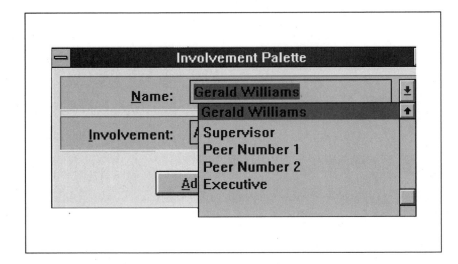

3. Click the ADD button at the bottom of the Modify Names box. This generates the Add Involvement Name box.

```
┌─────────────────────────────────────┐
│  ┌───────────────────────────────┐   │
│  │ ▬    Add Involvement Name     │   │
│  ├───────────────────────────────┤   │
│  │ New Involvement Name          │   │
│  │ ┌───────────────────────────┐ │   │
│  │ │ │                         │ │   │
│  │ └───────────────────────────┘ │   │
│  │                               │   │
│  │      ┌────────┐  ┌────────┐   │   │
│  │      │ Cancel │  │   OK   │   │   │
│  │      └────────┘  └────────┘   │   │
│  └───────────────────────────────┘   │
└─────────────────────────────────────┘
```

4. Enter the new name you want to use. The box accepts names of up to 50 characters including spaces.

5. The ADD button adds the new name to the master list in the Modify Names box. The CANCEL button returns you to the Involvement Editor screen without making any changes.

Other methods exist to build and modify lists.

Using the Keyboard

1. Call the CREATE pull-down menu in the Milestone Planner screen command bar by entering (ALT) (T).

2. Select INVOLVEMENTS from the pull-down menu by keying (I). This creates the Modify Names screen.

3. (TAB) to highlight the ADD button at the bottom of the Modify Names box and hit (ENTER). This generates the Add Involvement Name box.

4. Enter the new name you want to use. The box accepts up to 50 characters including spaces.

5. Highlight the ADD button and hit (ENTER) to add the new name to the master list in the Modify Names box. Highlight the CANCEL button and hit (ENTER) to return to the Involvement Editor screen without making any changes.

Other methods exist to build and modify lists.

USING THE INVOLVEMENT PALETTE

The Involvement Palette allows you to easily identify people and involvement levels without rekeying names and responsibilities for each person. However, you should fill in all the names and set the list of proper involvements. Then you can begin to link the names to involvements, creating involvement pairs that link to the Sub Milestone currently active on the Milestone Planner screen.

Using the Mouse

1. Click on PLANNER in the Milestone Planner command bar. A pull-down menu appears.

File	Edit	Planner	Create

Milestone Palette...
Assumption Palette...
Involvement Palette...

Add   ▶
Delete   ▶
Rename   ▶

Show Finding...
Primary Responsibility...

2. Select Involvement Palette from the pull-down menu. The Involvement Palette will display.

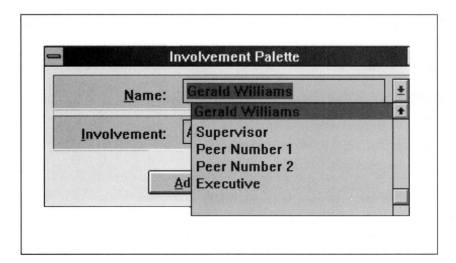

You also can click twice on the Involvements area of the Milestone Planner screen to move directly to the Involvement Palette.

3. Click on the pull-down menu box at the right of the Name box. All available names will be listed alphabetically.

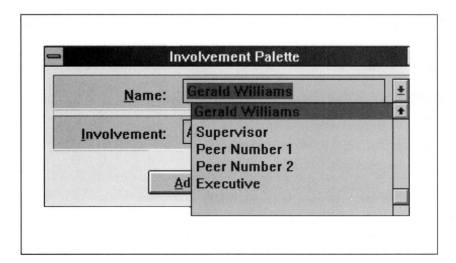

4. Select the name from the list. You can use the scroll bar to browse the list or enter the first letter of the name you want. The highlight jumps to the first entry that starts with that letter.

5. Click on the pull-down menu box at the right of the Involvements box. All available Involvements are listed alphabetically.

6. Select the involvement from the list. You can use the scroll bar to browse the list or enter the first letter of the name you want. The highlight jumps to the first entry that starts with that letter.

Using the Keyboard

1. Call the PLANNER pull-down menu in the Milestone Planner command bar by entering ⟨ALT⟩ ⟨P⟩.

2. Select Involvement Palette from the pull-down menu by keying ⟨I⟩. The Involvement Palette displays.

3. Highlight the name you want by viewing the names one at a time and using the cursor (arrow) keys.

4. ⟨TAB⟩ to highlight the Involvements box and view the Involvements one at time using the arrow keys. All available Involvements are listed alphabetically.

APPLYING THE INVOLVEMENT PAIR

Once the involvement pair is identified on the Involvement Palette, you can link them to the active Major Milestone or Sub Milestone by clicking on the ADD button or tabbing to the ADD button and hitting the enter key.

REPORTING

Milestone Planning for Successful Ventures offers a variety of prescribed reports that allow you to report or graph the project's or venture's progress. You can create these reports quickly and easily; they are designed from real-world needs identified by Educational Software.

CREATING A REPORT

Using the Mouse

1. Click on CREATE in the Milestone Planner screen command bar. A pull-down menu appears.

File	Edit	Planner	Create

Milestone Templates...	Ctrl+M
Assumptions...	Ctrl+A
Involvements...	Ctrl+I
Reports...	Ctrl+R

---

2. Select REPORT from the pull-down menu. This calls the Create & Modify Reports screen.

Create & Modify Reports - []

| File | Edit | Report | | Help |

Report Text

```
-----------------------------------------------------------------
Milestone Report:    Basic
Date-Time Stamp:     Friday, May 28, 1994 - 06:06 AM
-----------------------------------------------------------------


*****************************************************************
· A. Concept/Product Test
```

Cost   Time   Gantt

Cancel   OK

---

3. Click on FILE in the Create & Modify Reports command bar. This generates another pull-down menu.

File	Edit	Report			Create & Modify Reports
New...		Ctrl+N			
Open...		Ctrl+O			
Save		Ctrl+S			
Save As...					
Print		Ctrl+P			
Printer Setup					
Exit Editor		Ctrl_X			

4. Select NEW from the pull-down menu. The New Milestone Report screen displays with an alphabetical listing of all available Milestone Sets.

New Milestone Report

Available Documents

A Basic Project
A Second Milestone Set
A Third Milestone Set
Basic
General Milestones
Master Milestones
Milestones/Mac&Zenas
The Other Project
Venture Milestones

OK

Cancel

Settings...

5. Highlight the Milestone Set you want to use for the report by clicking on the selection with the mouse. The scroll bar to the right of the box listing the Milestone Sets can be used to review the list. As an option, you can key the first letter of the Milestone

Set you need. The highlight moves to the first Milestone Set that begins with that letter.

6. Click on the OK button to generate the text report. The CANCEL button returns you to the Milestone Planner screen without creating a report.

 Using the Keyboard

1. Call the CREATE pull-down menu from the Milestone Planner screen by keying ALT   T .

2. Select REPORT from the pull-down menu and call the Create & Modify Reports screen by entering R . **Note:** You can speed the process by entering CTRL   R from the Milestone Planner screen.

3. Generate the FILE pull-down menu by entering ALT   F .

4. Select NEW from the pull-down menu by keying N . The New Milestone Report screen displays all available Milestone Sets alphabetically.

5. Highlight the Milestone Set you want to use for the report by cursoring through the list. As an option, you can key the first letter of the Milestone Set you need. The highlight moves to the first Milestone Set that begins with that letter. To move to the Name of New Report box, hit the TAB . **Note:** For a shortcut, you can enter CTRL   N from the Create & Modify Reports screen.

6. To generate the text report, key ENTER .

If you tab to highlight the CANCEL button and key ENTER , you return to the Milestone Planner screen without creating a report.

USING SETTINGS

Settings allow you to select which fields and elements you want to include in the report. This gives you the power you need to customize the report and generate regular updates at the click of a button.

Using the Mouse

1. Select REPORT from the pull-down menu. This calls the Create & Modify Reports screen.

```
┌──────────────────────────────────────────────────────────┐
│ ▭              Create & Modify Reports - []               │
│  File  Edit  Report                                  Help │
│ ┌────────────────────────────────────────────────────────┐│
│ │Report Text                                              ││
│ │ ─────────────────────────────────────────────────── ▲ ││
│ │                                                        ││
│ │ Milestone Report:    Basic                             ││
│ │ Date-Time Stamp:     Friday, May 28, 1994 - 06:06 AM   ││
│ │ ─────────────────────────────────────────────────      ││
│ │                                                        ││
│ │ ****************************************************    ││
│ │                                                        ││
│ │ - A. Concept/Product Test                           ▼ ││
│ │ ◄                                                  ► ││
│ │ Cost                    Time              Gantt       ││
│ │ [▮▮] [⟋] [◔] [⩗]  [▮▮] [⟋] [◔] [⩗]    [▤]        ││
│ │                              [Cancel]   [OK]          ││
│ └────────────────────────────────────────────────────────┘│
└──────────────────────────────────────────────────────────┘
```

2. Click on FILE in the Create & Modify Reports command bar. This generates a pull-down menu.

```
┌──────────────────────────────────────────────────────────┐
│ ▭                          Create & Modify Reports        │
│  File   Edit   Report                                     │
│ ┌──────────────────────────────┐                         │
│ │ New...              Ctrl+N    │                         │
│ │ Open...             Ctrl+O    │                         │
│ │ Save                Ctrl+S    │                         │
│ │ Save As...                    │                         │
│ ├──────────────────────────────┤                         │
│ │ Print               Ctrl+P    │                         │
│ │ Printer Setup                 │                         │
│ ├──────────────────────────────┤                         │
│ │ Exit Editor         Ctrl_X    │                         │
│ └──────────────────────────────┘                         │
└──────────────────────────────────────────────────────────┘
```

3. If you need to start a report from scratch, select NEW from the pull-down menu. The New Milestone Report screen displays with an alphabetical listing of all available Milestone Sets.

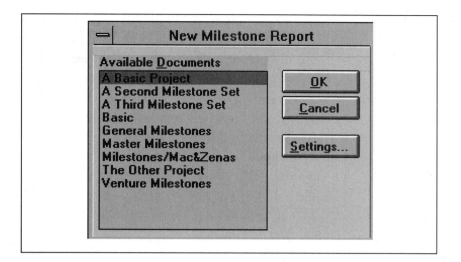

4. Highlight the Milestone Set you want to use for the report by clicking on the selection with the mouse. The scroll bar to the right of the box listing the Milestone Sets can be used to review the list. As an option, you can key the first letter of the Milestone Set you need. The highlight moves to the first Milestone Set that begins with that letter. Select the Milestone Set you want; then click on the Name of New Report box and enter the new report's name.

5. Click on the SETTINGS button. The Report Generator screen appears with a list of information elements that can be included in your report.

6. Select the elements you want to include in your report by clicking in the small box to the left of each information element. A check mark indicates that the element is selected; a blank box means the element will not appear in the final report.

7. If you want to include all elements in the report, click the FULL REPORT button. You will notice that all boxes now hold a check mark except for the box titled w/o Sub Milestones. If you choose, you can now customize the full report by clicking on those elements that you do not want to include in your report.

8. Hit the OK button to generate the report and return to the New Milestone screen. The CANCEL button returns you to the New Milestone screen without recording your selections.

9. Select the OK button on the New Milestone screen to generate the report. The CANCEL button returns to the Create & Modify Reports screen.

At this point, the report appears in the Report Text box. The vertical and horizontal scroll bars are active and you can browse this report. The report is grouped by Major Milestones and lists all the assumptions, findings, and primary responsibilities (Involvements) for each Major Milestone. Additionally, it presents the planned and actual costs and time side-by-side (including dates) along with a calculated difference. This report summarizes the progress of the project in one, easy-to-read report. Sub Milestones appear under the Major Milestones using the same format to present their assumptions, findings, primary responsibilities, costs, and time.

 Using the Keyboard

Call the CREATE pull-down menu in the Milestone Planner command bar by keying (ALT) (T).

1. Select REPORT from the pull-down menu and call the Create & Modify Reports screen by entering (R).

2. Generate the FILE pull-down menu in the Create & Modify Reports command bar with (ALT) (F).

3. If you need to start a report from scratch, select NEW from the pull-down menu by entering (N). The New Milestone Report screen displays all available Milestone Sets

ly.

4. Highlight the Milestone Set you want to use for the report by clicking on the selection with the mouse. The scroll bar to the right of the box listing the Milestone Sets can be used to review the list. As an option, you can key the first letter of the Milestone Set you need. The highlight moves to the first Milestone Set that begins with that letter. Select the Milestone Set you want; then click on the Name of New Report box and enter the new report's name.

5. To load the file, hit (ENTER).

6. Tab until the SETTINGS button is highlighted and hit (ENTER). The Report Generator screen appears with a list of information elements that can be included in your report.

7. Select the elements you want to include in your report by tabbing to the information you want and hitting the space bar. A check mark indicates that the element is selected; a blank box means the element will not appear in the final report.

8. If you want to include all elements in the report, tab to highlight the FULL REPORT button and press enter. You will notice that all boxes now hold a check mark except for the box titled w/o Sub Milestones. If you choose, you can now customize the full report by tabbing to those elements that you do not want to include in your report and hitting the (SPACE) bar.

9. Tab until the OK button is highlighted and press (ENTER) to generate the report and return to the New Milestone screen. If you highlight the CANCEL button and hit (ENTER), you return to the New Milestone screen without recording your selections.

10. Highlight the OK button on the New Milestone screen and key (ENTER) to generate the report. Again, if you highlight the CANCEL button and hit (ENTER), you return to the Create & Modify Reports screen.

EDITING THE REPORT

Once a report displays in the screen, you can click in the box to activate a cursor. Like most text editing systems, you can enter any text you want from the keyboard. Also, you can highlight characters, words, and sets of words by holding the left mouse button down while you drag the cursor across the characters you want to highlight. Once highlighted, you can edit that section by clicking on EDIT (ALT) (E) in the command bar (which generates a pull-down menu). The following functions are available:

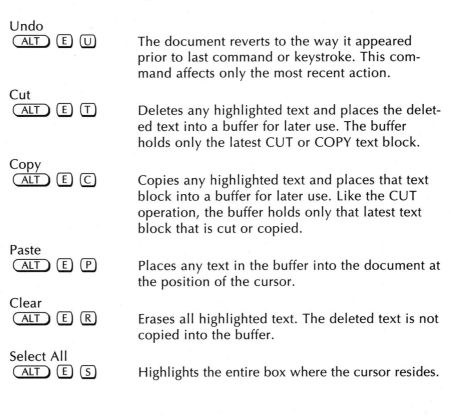

Undo
(ALT) (E) (U)   The document reverts to the way it appeared prior to last command or keystroke. This command affects only the most recent action.

Cut
(ALT) (E) (T)   Deletes any highlighted text and places the deleted text into a buffer for later use. The buffer holds only the latest CUT or COPY text block.

Copy
(ALT) (E) (C)   Copies any highlighted text and places that text block into a buffer for later use. Like the CUT operation, the buffer holds only that latest text block that is cut or copied.

Paste
(ALT) (E) (P)   Places any text in the buffer into the document at the position of the cursor.

Clear
(ALT) (E) (R)   Erases all highlighted text. The deleted text is not copied into the buffer.

Select All
(ALT) (E) (S)   Highlights the entire box where the cursor resides.

EXITING THE EDITOR

It is important that you exit the editor correctly and then save all changes. This ensures that you will be able to reuse all the modifications when you come back to the report generator.

Using the Mouse

1. Click on FILE in the Create & Modify Reports command bar. This generates a pull-down menu.

	Create & Modify Reports
File **Edit** **Report**	
New... Ctrl+N	
Open... Ctrl+O	
Save Ctrl+S	
Save As...	
Print Ctrl+P	
Printer Setup	
Exit Editor Ctrl_X	

2. Select EXIT EDITOR from the pull-down menu. This returns you to the Milestone Planner screen.

Note: The system does not check to see if you have saved all your changes to the report. You must, therefore, be careful to save the latest version of the file before exiting the editor.

Using the Keyboard

Call the FILE pull-down menu in the Create & Modify Reports command bar by entering ⌨ALT⌨ ⌨F⌨ .

GENERATING CHARTS

Charts are the easiest way to compare a venture's or project's progress against its goals. Two classes of comparisons—cost and time—can be created using the graphing module. This module also supports a Gantt Chart that shows Major Milestones.

Using the Mouse

Once a report is active:

1. Click REPORT in the Create & Modify Reports command bar. This yields a pull-down menu.

```
┌──────────────────────────────────────────────────────────┐
│                                                            │
│                                                            │
│  ▬               Create & Modify Reports                   │
│  ─────────────────────────────────────────────────────    │
│   File   Edit   Report                                     │
│  ──────────────┬───────────────────────────┬──────────    │
│                │  Default Settings...       │              │
│                │                            │              │
│                │  Cost Graphs               │              │
│                │  Time Graphs               │              │
│                │  Gantt Chart               │              │
│                └───────────────────────────┘              │
│                                                            │
│                                                            │
└──────────────────────────────────────────────────────────┘
```

2. Select COST GRAPHS, TIME GRAPHS, or GANTT CHART from the pull-down menu. For the COST GRAPHS and TIME GRAPHS options, a submenu appears to the right.

```
┌──────────────────────────────────────────────────────────┐
│                                                            │
│                                                            │
│  ▬               Create & Modify Reports                   │
│  ─────────────────────────────────────────────────────    │
│   File   Edit   Report                                     │
│  ──────────────┬───────────────────────────┬──────────    │
│                │  Default Settings...       │              │
│                │                     ┌──────┴──────────┐   │
│                │  Cost Graphs        │  Pie Graph      │   │
│                │  Time Graphs        │  Bar Graph      │   │
│                │  Gantt Chart        │  Line Graph     │   │
│                └─────────────────────┤  Area Graph     │   │
│                                      └─────────────────┘   │
│                                                            │
└──────────────────────────────────────────────────────────┘
```

3. Regardless of your next selection, the Chart Characteristics screen will present your options. If you select the GANTT CHART option, it goes directly to this screen.

4. Select planned and/or actual data and specify whether you want a two-dimensional chart or a three-dimensional chart by clicking on the box to the left of each option. A bullet inside the box means the option is activated, while a blank box indicates that selection is not activated.

5. Click the OK button to display the graph. Click on the box in the upper left-hand corner to access the pull-down menu and select CLOSE from that menu to cancel this screen and return to the Create & Modify Report screen without creating a graph.

Once the graph displays, you can either minimize or close the graph using the pull-down screen menu accessed by clicking on the box to the left of the screen's title box.

An easier way to create graphs is through the graphic buttons at the bottom of the Report screen. Once a report is active:

```
┌──────────────────────────────────────────────────────────────┐
│  ┌─────────────────────────────────────────────────────────┐  │
│  │ ═       Create & Modify Reports - []                     │  │
│  │ File  Edit  Report                               Help    │  │
│  │ ┌───────────────────────────────────────────────────┐    │  │
│  │ │Report Text                                        ▲│    │  │
│  │ │──────────────────────────────────────────────────┐│    │  │
│  │ │Milestone Report:    Basic                        ││    │  │
│  │ │Date-Time Stamp:     Friday, May 28, 1994 - 06:06 AM││   │  │
│  │ │                                                  ─┘│    │  │
│  │ │***************************************************│    │  │
│  │ │· A. Concept/Product Test                         ▼│    │  │
│  │ │◄                                                 ►│    │  │
│  │ ├───────────────────────────────────────────────────┤    │  │
│  │ │Cost                 Time                    Gantt │    │  │
│  │ │ ███  ╱╲   ◕   ╱╲    ███  ╱╲   ◕   ╱╲    ┌──┐     │    │  │
│  │ │ ███ ╱  ╲  ◕   ╱  ╲  ███ ╱  ╲  ◕   ╱  ╲   │▭═│     │    │  │
│  │ │                                         └──┘     │    │  │
│  │ │                                 ┌────────┐ ┌────┐│    │  │
│  │ │                                 │ Cancel │ │ OK ││    │  │
│  │ │                                 └────────┘ └────┘│    │  │
│  │ └───────────────────────────────────────────────────┘    │  │
│  └─────────────────────────────────────────────────────────┘  │
└──────────────────────────────────────────────────────────────┘
```

1. Select the graphic you want by clicking on that graphic button. This generates the Chart Characteristics screen that presents your options.

2. Select planned and/or actual data and specify whether you want a two-dimensional chart or a three-dimensional chart by clicking on the box to the left of each option. A bullet inside the box means the option is activated; a blank box indicates that selection is not activated.

3. Click the OK button to display the graph. Click on the box in the upper left-hand corner to access the pull-down menu and select CLOSE from that menu to cancel this screen and return to the Create & Modify Report screen without creating a graph.

Using the Keyboard

Once a report is active:

1. Generate the REPORT pull-down menu in the Create & Modify Reports command bar by keying ⟨ALT⟩ ⟨R⟩.

2. Select either COST GRAPHS ⟨C⟩ or TIME GRAPHS ⟨T⟩ from the pull-down menu. A submenu appears to the right.

3. Choose PIE GRAPH, BAR GRAPH, LINE GRAPH, or AREA GRAPH (depending on the type of chart you want to display)

by moving the cursor to highlight the report you want from the submenu. The Chart Characteristics screen presents your options. Press (ENTER).

4. Select planned (P) and/or actual (A) data and specify whether you want a two-dimensional chart (2) or a three-dimensional chart (3) by entering the underlined character. A bullet inside the box means the option is activated, while a blank box indicates that selection is not activated.

5. (TAB) to highlight the OK button and hit (ENTER) to display the graph. Key (SPACE) to generate the pull-down menu in the upper left-hand corner. Enter (C) to cancel this screen and return to the Create & Modify Report screen without creating a graph.

Once the graph displays, you can either minimize or close the graph using the pull-down screen menu accessed by keying (ALT) (SPACE).

An easier way to create graphs is through the graphic buttons at the bottom of the Report screen. Once a report is active:

1. (TAB) to highlight the graphic you want and hit (ENTER). This generates the Chart Characteristics screen that presents your options.

2. Select planned (P) and/or actual (A) data and specify whether you want a two-dimensional chart (2) or a three-dimensional chart (3) by entering the underlined character. A bullet inside the box means the option is activated, while a blank box indicates that selection is not activated.

3. (TAB) to highlight the OK button and hit (ENTER) to display the graph. Key (SPACE) to generate the pull-down menu in the upper left-hand corner. Enter (C) to cancel this screen and return to the Create & Modify Report screen without creating a graph.

The buttons generate several charts, including a Gantt chart that is helpful in planning. Notice that each chart carries a series of labels across the top. These self-explanatory functions work by clicking on them with the mouse or using the Tab key to move between them. These tools are very helpful in customizing the look and character of your report.

Bar Chart

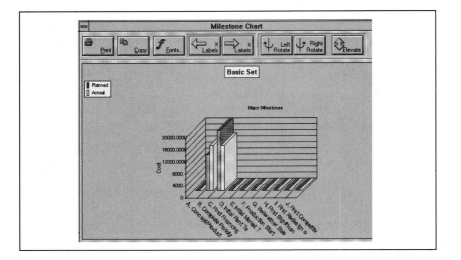

Line Chart

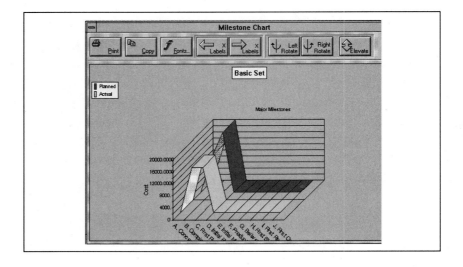

Pie Chart

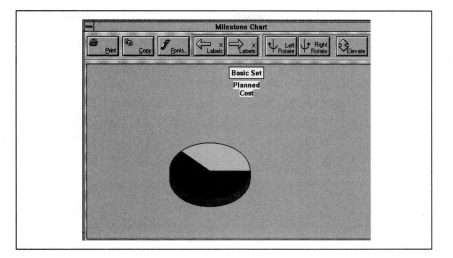

Area Chart

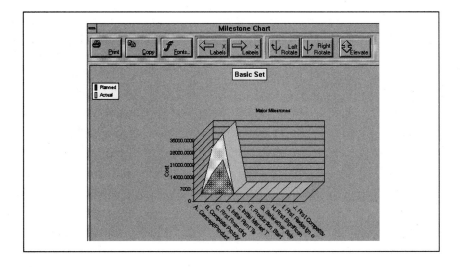

Gantt Chart

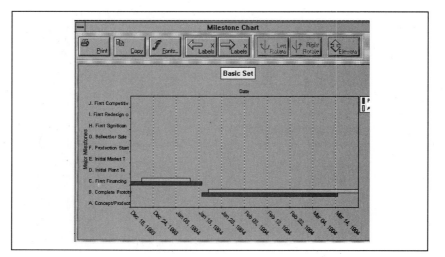

Using the Keyboard

Once a report is active:

1. Generate the REPORT pull-down menu in the Create & Modify Reports command bar by keying (ALT) (R).

2. Select either COST GRAPHS (C) or TIME GRAPHS (T) from the pull-down menu. A submenu appears to the right.

3. Choose PIE GRAPH, BAR GRAPH, LINE GRAPH, or AREA GRAPH (depending on the type of chart you want to display) by moving the cursor to highlight the report you want from the submenu. The Chart Characteristics screen presents your options. Press (ENTER).

4. Select planned (P) and/or actual (A) data and specify whether you want a two-dimensional chart (2) or a three-dimensional chart (3) by entering the underlined character. A bullet inside the box means the option is activated, while a blank box indicates that selection is not activated.

5. (TAB) to highlight the OK button and hit (ENTER) to display the graph. Key (SPACE) to generate the pull-down menu in the upper left-hand corner. Enter (C) to cancel this screen and return to the Create & Modify Report screen without creating a graph.

Once the graph displays, you can either minimize or close the graph using the pull-down screen menu accessed by keying ⦅ALT⦆ ⦅SPACE⦆ .

An easier way to create graphs is through the graphic buttons at the bottom of the Report screen. Once a report is active:

1. ⦅TAB⦆ to highlight the graphic you want and hit ⦅ENTER⦆ . This generates the Chart Characteristics screen that presents your options.

2. Select planned ⦅P⦆ and/or actual ⦅A⦆ data and specify whether you want a two-dimensional chart ⦅2⦆ or a three-dimensional chart ⦅3⦆ by entering the underlined character. A bullet inside the box means the option is activated, while a blank box indicates that selection is not activated.

5. ⦅TAB⦆ to highlight the OK button and hit ⦅ENTER⦆ to display the graph. Key ⦅ALT⦆ ⦅SPACE⦆ to generate the pull-down menu in the upper left-hand corner. Enter ⦅C⦆ to cancel this screen and return to the Create & Modify Report screen without creating a graph.

INDEX

Acquisition, 30–59
   financial statements of, 41–46, 54–55
   financing of, 36–37, 51, 53, 58–59
   new product development in, 37, 48, 50–51, 53
   opportunity for, 36–46
   restructuring of, 51, 53, 58–59
Action plan, 3–4
Adding
   involvements, 127–130
   Major and Sub Milestones, 115–117
Advantage, competitive, 21, 69
Analyses
   competition, 34–35
   consumer, 33–34
   ratio, 56
Area graphs, 144, 147, 148
Arrow keys, 118
Assumptions, 5–11, 21–23
   to cash flow statements, 78
   competitive, 8–9, 21
   defined, 4
   economic, 10–11
   environmental, 11
   financial, 21–22
   go/no go, 5–10
   high impact, 6–10
   identifying and defining, 6–11
   market and marketing, 7–8, 22–23, 102
   organizational, 9, 23
   product, 8, 23
   profit and loss, 21, 74–76
   relatively minor, 6
   replacing, 17
   supporting milestones, 122–124
   technology, 9–10, 23
Assumptions Palette, 124

Background, in business plan, 67–68
Backup functions, 101
Balance sheet, 42, 54
Bar graphs, 144, 146, 148
Bellwether sale, 15, 102
Block, Zenas, 1, 2, 99, 101
Break-even sales, 10
Budget, quantitative information on, 126
Business plan
   draft of, 65–78
   executive summary in, 67–68
   financial information in, 72, 73–78
   lack of, 26–28

   market in, 68–69
   operational description in, 69–72
   preparing, 13
   purpose of, 2
   rationale and method for, 3–4
   for return to profitability, 48
   table of contents of, 66

CANCEL button, 109, 111, 114, 115, 116, 117, 119, 129, 135, 138, 140
Case studies
   Enviromarine Corp., 84–95
   MaxRail, Ltd., 62–82
   Sandbox and Ting, 26–28
   Spice Kitchen, 30–59
Cash flow statement, 44, 77–78
Charts, 141–149
   closing, 143, 145
   Gantt, 142, 143, 145, 148
   generating, 141–149
   minimizing, 143, 145
   number of dimensions in, 145, 148, 149
   pie, 144, 147, 148
Clear command, 120, 121, 140
Coca–Cola Company, 10
Code Enforcement Citation, 58
Command bar, 101, 103, 104
Commands, editing, 120–121, 140
Competition
   analysis of, 34–35
   assumptions about, 8–9, 21
   in business plan, 69
   first competitive action, 16, 102
Competitive advantage, 21, 69
Concept test, 11–12, 101, 102
Consumer analysis, 33–34
Consumer behavior, 22
Copy command, 120, 140
Corporate strategy, 52
Cost
   projected, 75
   quantitative information on, 126
   as resource, 18
Cost graphs, 142, 144, 148
Create & Modify Reports screen, 133–134, 135, 142
Create Menu, 104, 117
Creating
   charts, 141–149
   documents, 107–111
   milestones, 106–111

reports, 133–135
Critical Path, 4–5
Critical path management (CPM) techniques, 98–99, 102
Critical path milestone planning, 5, 10
Cut command, 120, 140

Debt, restructuring, 51, 53, 58–59
Demand, for product, 22
Design, 15–16, 102
Distribution
    marketing and, 35
    in partnership, 73, 75–76
    See also Marketing
Documents
    creating, 107–111
    opening, 111–115
    saving, 112–113, 114–115
Draft, of business plan, 65–78

Economic assumptions, 10–11
Economic conditions, 32–33
Edit Menu, 104
Editing
    Findings, 124
    reports, 140
Enviromarine Corp. case study, 84–95
    financing, 87–90
    partnership arrangement, 84, 87
    product development, 84–90
    publicity and public relations, 92–95
Environmental assumptions, 11
Equipment
    inventory of, 39–40
    product redesign and, 15–16
    See also Technology
Executive summary, 67–68
Exiting
    Findings, 125
    reports, 141
Expenses
    operating, 45
    projected, 74–75
Exxon Corporation, 6, 11

Feasibility study, 13
File Menu, 104
Financial forecast, review of, 41
Financial information, in business plan, 72, 73–78
Financial statements, 41–46

balance sheet, 42, 54
cash flow, 44, 77–78
income statement, 43, 55
notes to, 46
profit and loss, 73–76
schedule of operating expenses, 45
Financing
    of acquisition, 36–37, 51, 53, 58–59
    assumptions about, 21–22
    final, 89–90
    first, 14, 87–89, 101
    of new venture, 14, 21–22, 87–90
    restructuring, 51, 53, 58–59
Findings, 124–125
Focus group, 12
Fraud, 49
FULL REPORT button, 138, 139
Funds
    as resource, 18
    source and uses of, 72
    See also Financing
Gantt charts, 142, 143, 145, 148
Go/no go assumption, 5–10
Graphs
    area, 144, 147, 148
    bar, 144, 146, 148
    cost, 142, 144, 148
    line, 144, 146, 148
    time, 142, 144, 148
    See also Charts

High impact assumptions, 6–10

Income statement, 43, 55
Industry, and individual company, 32–35, 48–49
Informal survey, 12, 78–81
Information
    financial, 72, 73–78
    quantitative, 126
Installation, 100–101
Insurance
    for new ventures, 81–82
    projected cost of, 75
Interest rates, assumptions about, 21
Interviews, 12
Inventory
    of equipment, 39–40
    management of, 52
Involvement, levels of, 18, 126–132
Involvement pair, 130, 132

Involvements Palette, 130–132

Keyboard
  adding involvements with, 129
  adding Major and Sub Milestones with, 117
  changing Milestone Template with, 120–121
  creating milestones with, 110–111
  creating reports with, 135
  exiting editor with, 141
  generating charts with, 144–145, 148–149
  installation with, 100–101
  opening documents with, 114–115
  saving Milestone Template with, 122
  selecting elements for inclusion in reports with,
    139–140
  selecting Major and Sub Milestones with,
    118–119
  using Involvements Palette with, 132
Knight, Russell M., 84n

Limited partnership, 67, 72, 73, 75–76, 81–82
Line graphs, 144, 146, 148

MacMillan, Ian, 99, 101
Maintenance
  deferred, 58
  projected cost of, 75
Major Milestones, 102, 105–106
  adding, 115–117
  order of listing, 109
  primary responsibility for, 125
  selecting, 106, 117–119
Management, 35
Margins
  assumptions about, 21
  high, 50, 52
Market
  assumptions about, 7–8, 22–23, 102
  in business plan, 68–69
  growth of, 69
  segmentation of, 22, 35
  size of, 23, 69
  target, 68–69
Market profile, 57
Market research, 12, 78–81
Market test, 14–15, 50, 101
Marketing
  assumptions about, 7–8
  distribution and, 35
  of new products, 14–15, 50–51, 53

MaxRail, Ltd. case study, 62–82
  business opportunity, 62–64
  business plan, 65–78
  business problems, 81–82
  financial statements, 72, 73–78
  market research, 78–81
McDiarmid, David, 84n
Media references, 95
Milestone(s), 11–16, 101–102
  assumptions supporting, 122–124
  creating, 106–111
  critical path, 5, 10
  defined, 4
  Major, 102, 105–106. *See also* Major Milestones
  order of listing, 109
  primary responsibility for, 125
  selecting, 106, 117–119
  Sub Milestones, 16, 102, 106. *See also* Sub
    Milestones
  test, 16
  universal, 11–17
Milestone Document. *See* Documents
Milestone Palette, 118–119
Milestone Planner screen, 103, 109
Milestone Planning Document, 112–113, 114–115
Milestone Planning for Successful Ventures pro-
    gram, 98–149
  adding Major and Sub Milestones, 115–117
  changing Milestone Template, 119–121
  command bar, 101, 103, 104
  creating documents, 107–111
  creating milestones, 106–111
  installing, 100–101
  opening documents, 111–115
  preparing to use, 99
  requirements for using, 99–100
  saving Milestone Template, 121–122
  selecting Major and Sub Milestones, 106,
    117–119
  Show Findings feature, 124
Milestone Set
  creating, 106–111
  naming, 108–109, 110
  scrolling through list of, 134–135
  selecting, 134, 136–137, 139
Milestone Template
  activating, 112, 114
  changing, 119–121
  saving, 121–122
Milestone Template Editor, 107–111

Minimizing charts, 143, 145
Mortgage, Purchase Money, 37, 49, 51
Mouse
   adding involvements with, 128–129
   adding Major and Sub Milestones with, 115–117
   changing Milestone Template with, 119–120
   creating milestones with, 107–109
   creating reports with, 133–135
   exiting editor with, 141
   generating charts with, 142–144
   installation with, 100
   opening documents with, 111–114
   saving Milestone Template with, 121–122
   selecting elements for inclusion in reports with,
      136–139
   selecting Major and Sub Milestones with,
      117–118
   using Involvements Palette with, 130–132

Name, of Milestone Set, 108–109, 110
Network options, 101
New products
   development of, 13–14, 37, 48, 50–51, 53,
      84–90
   investing in, 48
   marketing of, 14–15, 50–51, 53
   prototypes of, 13–14, 88–89, 101, 102
New ventures
   draft of business plan for, 65–78
   opportunity for, 26–28, 62–64, 86–87
   problems with, 2–3, 26–28, 81–82
Newsletters, 93–94
Notes
   to financial statements, 46
   promissory, 51, 58, 59

OPEC, 6, 11
Opening documents, 111–115
Operating expenses, schedule of, 45
Operational description, in business plan, 69–72
Opportunities, business
   for acquisitions, 36–46
   for new ventures, 26–28, 62–64, 86–87
Organizational assumptions, 9, 23

Palettes
   Assumptions, 124
   Involvements, 130–132
   Milestone, 118–119
Partnership

lack of business plan for, 26–28
limited, 67, 72, 73, 75–76, 81–82
in new product development, 84, 87
revenue distribution in, 73, 75–76
Paste command, 120, 140
People
   availability of, 23
   as resource, 17–18
   See also Users
Pie charts, 144, 147, 148
Pilot test, 14, 101
Plan
   action, 3–4
   critical path milestone, 5, 10
   See also Business plan
Planner Menu, 104, 117, 118
Planner screen, 103, 109
Planning Document, 112–113, 114–115
Preferences command, 101
Price, first significant change in, 15, 102
Printer options, 101
Product
   assumptions about, 8, 23
   demand for, 22
   development of, 13–14, 37, 48, 50–51, 53,
      84–90
   new. See New products
   purchase behavior and, 22
   quality of, 34
   redesign of, 15–16, 102
Product lines, 30–31
Product test, 12–13, 101, 102
Production start–up, 15, 101
Profit and loss assumptions, 21, 74–76
Profit and loss statement, 73–76
Profitability, plan for returning to, 48
Projections, 2, 74–75
Promissory note, 51, 58, 59
Property, deferred maintenance on, 58
Prototype, 13–14, 88–89, 101, 102
Publicity and public relations, 92–95
Purchase behavior, 22
Purchase Money Mortgage, 37, 49, 51

Quality, 34
Quantitative information, 126
Questionnaires, 12, 78–80
Quickstart. See Milestone Planning for Successful
      Ventures program

Ratio analysis, 56
Redirection, 15–16, 17, 102
Relatively minor assumptions, 6
Reports, 132–149
    charts for, 141–149
    creating, 133–135
    editing, 140
    exiting, 141
    saving, 141
    scrolling through, 138–139
    selecting elements for inclusion in, 135–140
Research, market, 12, 78–81
Resources, 17–19
    funds, 18
    people, 17–18
    time, 18–19
Responsibility, for milestones, 125
Restructuring, 51, 53, 58–59
Retail operations, 31
Revenue
    distribution of, in partnership, 73, 75–76
    projected, 74

Sandbox and Ting case study, 26–28
Saving
    documents, 112–113, 114–115
    Milestone Template, 121–122
    reports, 141
Schedules
    of operating expenses, 45
    quantitative information on, 126
Scrolling
    through list of Milestone Sets, 134–135
    through reports, 138–139
Segmentation, of market, 22, 35
Select All command, 120, 121, 140
Selecting
    elements for inclusion in reports, 135–140
    Milestone Set, 134, 136–137, 139
    milestones, 106, 117–119
SETTINGS button, 137, 139
Show Findings feature, 124
Social trends, 33
Spice Kitchen case study, 30–59
    acquisition opportunity, 36–46
    company background, 30, 49
    distribution and marketing, 35
    financial statements, 41–46, 54–55
    inventory management system, 52
    management, 35

market profile, 57
new product development, 37, 48, 50–51, 53
product lines, 30–31
ratio analysis, 56
restructuring, 51, 53, 58–59
retail operations, 31
spice industry, 32–35, 48–49
wholesale operations, 31–32
Stated assumption, 6
Statement, financial. *See* Financial statements
Statement of cash flow, 44, 77–78
Strategy, corporate, 52
Sub Milestones, 16, 102, 106
    adding, 115–117
    order of listing, 109
    primary responsibility for, 125
    selecting, 106, 117–119
Surveys, 12, 78–81

Target market, 68–69
Technology
    assumptions about, 9–10, 23
    computerized tracking system, 52
    product redesign and, 15–16
Templates. *See* Milestone Template
Test(s)
    concept, 11–12, 101, 102
    market, 14–15, 50, 101
    pilot, 14, 101
    product, 12–13, 101, 102
Test milestone, 16
Time
    assumptions about, 22
    as resource, 18–19
Time graphs, 142, 144, 148
Tracking system, computerized, 52

Unconscious assumption, 6
Undo command, 120, 140
Unstated assumption, 6
Users
    involvement of, 18, 126–132
    responsibility for milestones, 125

Valuation methods, 36–37, 38
Ventures. *See* New ventures

Wholesale operations, 31–32